Python for Beg

I0015910

Practical Introduction to Python Programming, Learn Fast and Well Python Programming Language With Examples and Practical Exercises

By

Kevin Cooper

Table of Contents

versions of the work, physical, digital, and audio unless express consent of the Publisher is provided beforehand. Any additional rights reserved.

Furthermore, the information that can be found within the pages described forthwith shall be considered both accurate and truthful when it comes to the recounting of facts. As such, any use, correct or incorrect, of the provided information will render the Publisher free of responsibility as to the actions taken outside of their direct purview. Regardless, there are zero scenarios where the original author or the Publisher can be deemed liable in any fashion for any damages or hardships that may result from any of the information discussed herein.

Additionally, the information in the following pages is intended only for informational purposes and should thus be thought of as universal. As befitting its nature, it is presented without assurance regarding its prolonged validity or interim quality. Trademarks that are mentioned are done without written consent and can in no way be considered an endorsement from the trademark holder.

7

Introduction

Congratulations on **purchasing** *Python for beginners,* and thank you for doing so.

The following chapters will discuss python programming language in detail with a lot of examples and hands-on exercises. We will also look at a lot of basic concepts in a way that beginners can understand and appreciate the robustness of Python when compared to other entry-level programming languages.

We will first start with a brief introduction that is followed by the installation of Python development environments in the native system. We will then introduce basic programming concepts like variables, operators, conditional and loop structures with a lot of examples to make the reader understand Python language in detail.

A lot of programming code is also given so that the reader can get a good idea on both theoretical and programmatical concepts.   Let us start our journey into the world of Python.

There are plenty of books on this subject on the market, so thanks again for choosing this one! Every effort was made to ensure it is full of as much useful information as possible. Please enjoy!

Chapter 1: Introduction to Python

This chapter introduces a brief knowledge to Python along with its history. This is quite basic and may involve theoretical background to make things easy for the beginners. We will also introduce an example program so that we can get a good starting feel for Python environment. Let us start for our very first chapter in this book.

What is Python?

Python is a dynamic explanatory programming language. Python is easy to learn and powerful and supports object-oriented and functional programming. Python can be used on multiple operating systems such as Windows and UNIX, while Python can be used on development platforms such as Java and. NET, so it is also called "beginners programming language." Python's simplicity and ease of use make the development process concise, especially suitable for rapid application development.

In the next section, we will discuss a few basic historical advancements that lead to the discovery of the Python programming language.

Python and its History

Python was developed by Guido van Rossum in 1989 and finally published in early 1991. Guido van Rossum used to be a member of the CWI Company and used the interpretive programming language ABC to develop applications. This language has many limitations in software development. Because he wants to complete some tasks in system management, he needs to acquire the system call capability provided by the operating system of the Amoeba machine.

Although Amoeba's special language can be designed to accomplish this task, van Rossum plans to design a more general programming language. Python language has been born for more than 20 years and is gradually developing into one of the mainstream programming languages. TIOBE has long occupied the eighth position in the ranking of programming languages.

Due to the dynamic nature of Python, program interpretation and execution are slower than compiled languages. However, with the continuous optimization of Python language, the continuous development of some projects such as PyCharm, and the continuous development of computer hardware technology, dynamic language has received more and more attention in the industrial field.

The representative languages include Python, Ruby, SmallTalk, Groovy, etc.

As we all know, Java is a recognized development language in the field of industrial applications. Java is easier to use than C++, and its internal structure is relatively simple. Python's syntax makes programming easier. Python can be used to write code that is more readable than Java.

With the advent of interpreters such as Jython, Python can be run on Java virtual machines. This way, Python can use Java rich application packages. Python is very similar to JavaScript, which is well known to readers. It is interpreted and executed, and its syntax structure has many similarities. JavaScript is the client script language on the browser side, and Python can also be used for Web development.

Python, as a scripting language, absorbs the advantages of Perl, react and other languages, which makes Python have React extensibility and Perl text parsing and matching capabilities. Python and Lisp also have similarities. Python can implement a functional programming model.

Python and Its Features

Programming languages are continuously developing, from the initial assembly language to the later C and Pascal languages, to the present C++, Java and other high-level programming languages. The difficulty of program design is decreasing. A set of standards has been formed for software development and design. Development is no longer a complicated task.

At first, only machine code can be used to write code, but now an IDE environment with good debugging function can be used to program. Python is developed in C, but Python no longer has complex data types such as pointers in C language. Python's simplicity greatly reduces software code and simplifies development tasks. Programmers no longer focus on grammatical features, but on the tasks that the program is to accomplish.

Python has many important features, and some of them are creative and paved for a boom in software development.

1. Object-oriented features

Object-oriented programming solves the complexity of structured programming and makes programming closer to real life. Structured programming mixes data and logic together, which is not convenient for program maintenance. Object-oriented programming abstracts the behaviors and attributes of objects and separates the behaviors and attributes but organizes them together reasonably.

Python language has strong object-oriented characteristics and simplifies the implementation of object-oriented. It eliminates object-oriented elements such as protection types, abstract classes, interfaces, etc., making the concept of object-oriented easier to understand.

2. Built-in data structure

Python provides some built-in data structures that implement functions similar to collection classes in Java. Python's data structure includes tuples, lists, dictionaries, collections, etc. The appearance of the built-in data structure simplifies the design of the program. Tuples are equivalent to "read-only" arrays, lists can be used as variable-length arrays, and dictionaries are equivalent to Hash Table types in Java.

3. Simplicity

Python has fewer keywords. It does not have semicolons, begin, end, etc. The code blocks are separated by spaces or tab indents. Python's code is simple, short, and easy to read. Python simplifies loop statements and can be read quickly even if the program structure is very complex.

4. Robustness

Python provides an exception handling mechanism that can catch exceptions in programs. In addition, Python's stack trace object can point out the location of the program error and the cause of the error. Exception mechanism can avoid unsafe exit and help programmers debug programs.

5. Cross-platform

Python is compiled into platform-related binary code before interpretation and execution. This approach is similar to Java, but Python's execution speed has increased. Python-written applications can run on different operating systems such as Windows, UNIX, Linux, etc. Python code written on one operating system can be ported to other operating systems with only a few modifications.

6. Scalability

Python is a language developed by C, so it can be extended by C, and new modules and classes can be added to Python. At the same time, Python can be embedded into projects developed in C and C++ languages to make the program have script language.

7. Dynamics

Python is similar to JavaScript, PHP, Perl, and other languages. It does not need to declare another variable. It can create a new variable by directly assigning a value.

8. Strongly Typed Languages

Python's variables are created to correspond to a type, which can determine the type of variables according to the content of the assignment expression. Python has built a mechanism to manage these variables internally. Different types of variables require type conversion.

9. Wide usage

Python language is applied to the database, network, graphic image, mathematical calculation, Web development, operating system expansion, and other fields. Python is supported by many third-party libraries. For example, the PIL library (now no longer maintained but replaced by Pillow) is used for image processing, the NumPy library is used for mathematical calculation, the WxPython library is used for GUI program design, and the Django framework is used for Web application program opening.

With this explanation, we can easily understand the advantages of python programming language offers. Next, we will give an example program that will let us introduce to Python language.

First Python Program

Python's source code file has "py" as the suffix. Next, write a simple Python program to create a file named sampleprogram.py to output the string "This is a whole new world."

Code is here:

```
if __name__ =="__main__":

print (" This is a whole new world")
```

Code Description:

The first line of code is equivalent to the main () function in C language and is the entrance of Python program. The second line of code uses the print statement to output the string "This is a whole new world."

The output is shown below:

This is a whole new world

Python's print statement is used to output the contents of the string, that is, to output the contents in double quotation marks to the console. Python's input and output are realized through "stream." The above print statement outputs the contents of the string to the standard output stream, that is, to the console. Streams can also output results to files, printers, etc.

Python programs are very simple to run, and the command format is as follows.

Command is here:

python filepath samplefilename.py

Where samplefilename.py represents python's source code file, filepath represents the path where samplefilename.py is located. Enter the command shown in the DOS window and run the file samplo.py.

This mode of operation is not intuitive enough and is not convenient for program debugging. Later, we will explain how to run Python programs in editors like Edit Plus and development tool PyCharm.

In the next section, we will describe the python development environment in detail.

Building Development Environment

The installation and configuration of Python development environment are very simple. Python can be installed and developed on multiple platforms. IPython is a very popular, powerful, and easy-to-use Python installation package. This section describes the installation of IPython and the use of Python interactive command lines.

Python download and installation

Python is installed by default on UNIX systems, Python's executable files are installed in the /usr/local/bin directory, and library files are installed in the /usr/local/python directory.

Although Python2 and Python3 are installed by default, Python in the terminal defaults to Python2, which is currently generally Python2.7.5. To use Python3, you need to enter python3 in the terminal or modify the default version. In a Windows environment, Python can be installed in any directory.

Readers can download Python3.3 from the official website www.python.org, which provides Python installation software for different operating systems such as Windows and UNIX.

Users can also install IPython interactive shell, which is much easier to use than the default terminal, supports automatic indentation, and has many useful functions and functions built-in. The address of its official website is http://ipython.org. It can be used on any operating system.

Windows users need to install Anaconda before installing IPython. Anaconda is an installation management program, which can be used to complete Python upgrade and other operations easily, and it has a lot of Python libraries, and its download address can be easily found out from the internet. Select the appropriate version of the user's machine and install it.

After the installation is completed, the user will find that in addition to the system default cmd.exe, there are more Anaconda Command Prompt terminals. The user can directly use the terminal or use the system default cmd.exe. After opening the terminal, enter Python and press enter, you may find that python version is 2.7.5 or something other than Python3.X we want. It doesn't matter.

Open any terminal and enter the following command:

update anaconda

create −n py3k python=versionnumber anaconda

During the installation process, there will be some prompts. Enter Y and press Enter. At this point, you can see information about a series of Python libraries installed. After the installation is completed, reopen the terminal and enter the following command:

activate py3k # This activates the interpreter in your system

Then enter iPython in the terminal, and the python version information and IPython version information will be displayed, and an interactive command window will be launched.

Since the current version supported by Anaconda defaults to Python2.7, you need to switch to py3k every time you want to use Python3.3. You can enter help in the IPython interactive environment to view help information.

Use of Interactive Command Line

After IPython is successfully installed, Anaconda can choose to use its own terminal or system terminal. After entering the terminal, input ipython to start the interactive environment. If you are using native python, you can start the command line program by simply entering Python and entering the command interface.

Through the command line, you can directly input statements to the interpreter and output the running results of the program. The Python program can be entered at the prompt in the command line window. The following uses the print statement to output the string "This is our world," as shown.

Of course, you can also enter multiple lines of Python code in the command line window. Next, enter the code in sampleexample.py into the command line window. After inputting the last line of the program, press enter twice to finish the program and output the running result of the program, as shown.

Note if you want to exit the interactive command line, enter exit and press enter. In the next section, we will introduce IDE tools such as Pycharm.

Python Development Tools

Python is rich in development tools, with many powerful IDE (Integrated Development Environment) tools, such as Komodo, PythonWin, Eclipse, PyCharm, etc. These tools not only support graphical operations but also have editing, debugging, and other functions.

In addition, the text editor can also be used as a Python development environment, such as Edit Plus, Vi, etc. PyCharm is a Python IDE developed by JetBrains. It has powerful functions and recently released an open-source community version, which is very suitable for learning.

Use of PyCharm

PyCharm is a cross-platform IDE that is very easy to use. It is developed in Java. It has a paid version and a community free version. This book will use the community free version. You can install it after downloading. After the installation is completed, running the program for the first time will require setting a theme, etc. You can choose to skip this step or choose yourself.

After setting up, restart, you can enter the program. Because it is an IDE, you first need to create a project, and then you will need to set up a Python path step by step, according to the requirements.

Note: If Anaconda is used, you need to select python.exe in py3k under envs directory. Otherwise, the default Python2.7 version 2.7 will be used.

PyCharm has its own Python command line interactive Terminal, which can easily run code and do related tests. Move the mouse to the lower-left corner and click the TERMINAL button to open it, which is very convenient.

Click the [File] | [New] menu and select the corresponding file type to create a new file and write a Python program in it. Now start to create hello_world.py file, select the Run command in the [Run] menu or press Alt+Shift after writing +F10 key combination can run the code.

In addition, PyCharm also supports advanced functions such as quick jump, code refactoring, code testing, version control, debugging, etc. Next, we will talk about the Eclipse development environment.

Introduction of Eclipse IDE

Eclipse is an integrated development environment for Java development and an open-source project. Eclipse is very extensible. Eclipse can not only be used as the IDE of Java but also develop a large number of plug-ins to support other applications.

For types of languages, such as C, C++, Python, PHP, etc., if you want to develop Python on the Eclipse platform, you need to download PyDev. The easy Eclipse website provides various plug-in downloads of Eclipse and can obtain Easy Eclipse for Python, which runs separately.

Eclipse is very powerful, and it realizes intelligent functions such as the syntax highlighting, code prompting, and code completion of Python code. In addition, Eclipse provides more powerful debugging capabilities than PythonWin, and also supports Jython, Pyunit, team development, and other functions.

In Eclipse, source code is organized into a project. The structure of the Eclipse user interface is divided into a View and an Editor. Examples of views and editors include source code outline view, Java source code editor, Python source code editor, and file system navigation view.

Eclipse user interface package

Views are a set of windows that are usually used when performing some type of activity. The standard views in Eclipse include Debug, Java Browsing, Java, Java Type Hierarchy, Plug-in Development, CVS Repository Exploring, Resource, and Install/ Update. Easy Eclipse for Python provides a Pydev view. When the debugging mode is started, Eclipse automatically switches to debug view.

Note

Python needs to be installed on your computer before Pydev can be installed.

Configuration of Edit Plus Editor Environment

Python can also be developed using an editor. For example, the text editing software Edit Plus can also become Python's editing and execution environment, and even be used for debugging programs. Edit Plus has functions such as syntax highlighting and code automatic indenting.

Here's how to configure it:

The development environment of Edit Plus editor.

1. Add Python Groups

a) Run Edit Plus, select [Tools] | [Configure User Tools] to open the [Parameters] dialog box. Click the [Add Tool] button and select the [Program] command in the pop-up menu. The name of the newly-created group is named python.

b) Enter Python in the [Menu Text] text box, enter the installation path of Python in the [Command] text box, enter $(FileName) in the [Parameters] text box, and enter $(FileDir) in the [Start Directory] text box.

c) Check the [Capture Output] option, and the output result of the Python program will be displayed in the output column of EditPlus. Otherwise, a command line window will pop up after running the Python program and output the result to the command line.

d) Click the [OK] button to create a new python file. Python options will appear under the [Tools] menu. Click this option, or use the shortcut ctrl+1 to transport

Line Python program.

2. Set Python Highlight and Auto Complete

Edit Plus can not only be used as Python's development environment but also supports Java, C#, PHP, HTML and other types of languages. Different languages have different forms of grammatical highlighting and automatic completion. In order to realize grammar highlighting and automatic completion, two characteristic files need to be downloaded.

After downloading, extract the files python.acp and python.stx to the installation directory of EditPlus. Files with acp suffix represent automatically completed feature files, and files with stx suffix represent feature files with syntax highlighted. These feature files need to be set in EditPlus before writing Python code.

(1) Select [File] | [Settings and Syntax] option, select [python] option in the [File Type] list, enter python in the [Description] text box, and click on

Enter py in the text box [extension].

(2) In the Settings and Grammar tab, enter the path of python.stx in the Grammar File text box and python.acp in the Auto Complete text box.

(3) Python syntax does not use begin, end or {,} to distinguish code blocks, but uses colon and code indentation to distinguish the hierarchical relationship between codes. Click the [tab/indent] button to open the [tab and indent] dialog box and set the indentation method of Python code.

When using IDE tools, entering colon codes will automatically indent, and this function can also be set with Edit Plus. Enter the number of spaces in the Tabs and Indents text boxes respectively, generally set to Select the [Start Auto Indent] option, enter ":" in the [Start Auto Indent] option, and click the [OK] button to save the settings.

(4) Click the [Function Model] button to open the [Function Model] dialog box, as shown. In the [Function Model Regular Expression] text box, enter [\t]*def[\t].+:. Click [OK] to save the settings.

At this point, the Python development environment for Edit Plus has been set up. Edit Plus can also create templates for Python files, and code can be written on the basis of the templates each time a Python file is created. Py's content is as follows.

#! /usr/bin/python

[Code Description]

The first line of code enables Python programs to run on UNIX platforms.

Note that in Edit Plus, you can view the list of functions in the current Python file by using the shortcut Ctrl+F11. You need to save the Python program before running it. Next, use Edit Plus to write a Python program and output the result.

Python Under Different Platforms

Java and .NET are two mature development platforms in the industry. Python can be used on these two development platforms, and Python can also be extended with Java and C#.

1. Jython

Jython is a Python parser written entirely in Java. Although the implementation and performance of Jython interpreter are still somewhat different from Python interpreter, Jython makes Python fully applicable under the Java development platform.

Jython enables Python programs to run on Java virtual machines while Python can access libraries and packages under Java. Jython also provides a perfect scripting environment for Java. Python can be used as an implementation language for middle-tier services in Java applications. Jython enables Java to extend Python modules, which in turn can be used to write Java applications.

2. IronPython

Iron Python is a Python implementation on the .NET platform. Iron Python provides an interactive console that supports dynamic compilation. It enables Python programmers to access all. NET libraries and is fully compatible with the Python language. Iron Python must provide support for .NET version 2.0. The appearance of Iron Python makes it possible to write

Python code under the .NET platform and call the rich .NET class library framework.

By this, we have explained a lot of basic concepts about Python. This chapter explained Python's history, features, and development environment. This chapter focused on the settings of the Python development environment, the features of IDE tools such as PyCharm and Eclipse, and the settings of Edit Plus editor. The next chapter will learn Python's basic syntax, including Python's file types, coding rules, data types, expressions, etc.

Let us dive into the next chapter where we will start discussing variables and data types in detail which are called as basic building blocks of any programming language.

Chapter 2: Variables and Constants in Python

This chapter on a whole level will introduce a lot of basic concepts that programming languages deal with. We will be discussing concepts like variables and data types with programmatical examples in the coming sections. Let us start diving into the world of variables in Python.

The most basic data processing objects in programming languages are constants and variables. Their main purpose is to store data for various calculations and processing in programs. In this chapter, we will discuss Python's basic data processing functions such as data types, variables, and constants, and introduce beginners to the basic syntax they need when writing small applications.

Why Variables are needed?

For any programming language, the basic part is to store the data in memory and process it. No matter what kind of operation we are going to perform, we must have the object of operation. It is difficult for a skillful woman to cook without rice. In Python language, constants and variables are the main ones. In fact, both of them are identification codes used by program designers to access data contents in memory.

The biggest difference between the two is that the contents of variables will change with the execution of the program, while the contents of constants are fixed forever. In the process of program execution, it is often necessary to store or use some data. For example, if you want to write a program to calculate the mid-term exam results, you must first input the students' results, and then output the total score, average score and ranking after calculation. This chapter describes how to store and access this data.

Variable Naming and Assignment

In a program, program statements or instructions tell the computer which Data to access and execute step by step according to the instructions in the program statements. These data may be words or numbers. What we call variable is the most basic role in a programming language, that is, a named memory unit allocated by the compiler in programming to store changeable data contents.

The computer will store it in "memory" and take it out for use when necessary. In order to facilitate identification, it must be given a name. We call such an object "variable."

For example:

> > firstsample = 3

>>>second sample= 5

> > > result = firstsample+secondsample

In the above program statement, firstsample, secondsample, result are variables, and number 3 is the variable value of firstsample. Since the capacity of memory is limited, in order to avoid wasting memory space, each variable will allocate memory space of different sizes according to requirements, so "Data Type" is used to regulate it.

Variable declaration and assignment

Python is an object-oriented language, all data are regarded as objects, and the method of an Object reference is also used in variable processing. The type of variable is determined when the initial value is given, so there is no need to declare the data type in advance. The value of a variable is assigned with "=" and beginners easily confuse the function of the assignment operator (=) with the function of "equal" in mathematics. In programming languages, the "=" sign is mainly used for assignment.

The syntax for declaring a variable is as follows:

variable name = variable value

e.g.

number = 10.

The above expression indicates that the value 10 is assigned to the variable number. In short, in Python language, the data type does not need to be declared in advance when using a variable, which is different from that in C language, which must be declared in advance before using a variable. Python interpretation and operation system will automatically determine the data type of the variable according to the value of the variable given or set.

For example, the data type of the above variable number is an integer. If the content of the variable is a string, the data type of the variable is a string.

Variable naming rules

For an excellent programmer, readability of program code is very important. Although variable names can be defined by themselves as long as they conform to Python's regulations, when there are more and more variables, simply taking variables with letter names such as abc will confuse people and greatly reduce readability.

Considering the readability of the program, it is best to name it according to the functions and meanings given by variables. For example, the variable that stores height is named "Height" and the variable that stores weight is named "Weight." Especially when the program scale is larger, meaningful variable names will become more important.

For example, when declaring variables, in order to make the program readable, it is generally used to start with lowercase letters, such as score, salary, etc. In Python, variable names also need to conform to certain rules. If inappropriate names are used, errors may occur during program execution. Python is a case-sensitive language. In other words, number and Number are two different variables. Variable names are not limited in length.

Variable names have the following limitations: the first character of a variable name must be an English letter, underlined "_" and cannot be a number. Subsequent characters can match other upper- and lower-case English letters, numbers, underlined "_," and no space character is allowed. You cannot use Python's built-in reserved words (or keywords).

Although Python version 3. X supports foreign language variable names; it is recommended that you try not to use words to name variables. On the one hand, it is more troublesome to switch input methods when inputting program code. On the other hand, the reading of program code will not be smooth. The so-called reserved word usually has special meaning and function, so it will be reserved in advance and cannot be used as a variable name or any other identifier name.

The following is an example of a valid variable name:

pageresponse

fileName4563

level

Number_dstance

The following is an example of an invalid variable name:

2_sample

for

$levelone

The user name learning classroom uses the help () function to query Python reserved word. The help () function is Python's built-in function. If you are not sure about the method and property usage of a specific object, you can use the help () function to query.

The Python reserved words mentioned above can be viewed by using the help () function. As long as "help ()" is executed, the help interactive mode will be entered. In this mode, the instructions to be queried will be input, and the relevant instructions will be displayed.

We can continue to input the instructions we want to query in help mode. When we want to exit help interactive mode, we can input Q or quit. You can also take parameters when entering the help () command, such as help ("keywords "), Python will directly display help or description the information without entering help interactive mode. Although Python uses dynamic data types, it is very strict in data processing, and its data type is "strong type."

For example:

> > > firstsample = 5

>>> secondsample= "45"

> > > print (firstsample+secondsample) # shows that TypeError variable firstsample is of numeric type and variable secondsample is of string type.

Some programming languages will convert the type unconsciously and automatically convert the value A to the string type, so firstsample+secondsample will get 545. Python language prohibits different data types from operating, so executing the above statement obviously Indicates information about the wrong type.

There is a difference between "strongly typed" and "weakly typed" in the data types of strong and weak type programming languages in small classrooms. One of the trade-offs is the safety of data type conversion. The strong type has a strict inspection for data type conversion. Different types of operations must be explicitly converted, and programs will not automatically convert. For example, Python and Ruby prefer strong types.

However, most weak type programming languages adopt Implicit Conversion. If you don't pay attention to it, unexpected type conversion will occur, which will lead to wrong execution results. JavaScript is a weak type of programming language.

Static Type and Dynamic Type

When Python is executed, the way to determine the data type belongs to "dynamic type."

What is the dynamic type?

The data types of programming languages can be divided into "Statically-Typed" and "Dynamically-Typed" according to the type checking method.

1. Static types are compiled with the type checked first, so the variables must be explicitly declared before they are used. The types of variables cannot be arbitrarily changed during execution. Java and C are such programming languages. For example, the following C language program statement declares that the variable number is of int integer type, and the initial value of the variable is set to 10. When we assign "apple" to number again, an error will occur, because "apple" is a string, and compilation will fail due to type discrepancy during compilation.

int firstsample = 10

firstsample = "apple"

#Error:

Types do not match

2. Dynamic types are compiled without prior type checking, and data types are determined according to variable values during execution. Therefore, there is no need to declare types before variables are used. The same variable can also be given different types of values, and Python is a dynamic type. For example, the following program statement declares the variable number and sets the initial value to the integer 10. When we assign the string apple to number, the type will be automatically converted.

firstsample= 10

firstsample= "love"

Print (firstsample)

output string love

Python has a Garbage Collection mechanism. When the object is no longer in use, the interpreter will automatically recycle and free up memory space. In the above example, when the integer object number is reassigned to another string object, the original integer object will be deleted by the interpreter. If the object is determined not to be used, we can also delete it by using the "del" command with the following syntax:

del object name

For example:

> > number = "apple"

> > > print(number) # output apple

> > > del number # deletes string object number

> > > print(number) #Error: number does not define the execution result.

Since the variable number has been deleted, if the number variable is used again, an undefined error message for the variable will appear.

Python's Numeric Data Types

Python's numeric data types are integer (int), floating-point number (float), and bool. The usage of these numeric types is explained one by one below.

The integer data type is used to store data without a decimal point, which has the same meaning as mathematics, such as -1, -2, -100, 0, 1, 2, 100, etc.

There are two types of integers in Python 2.x, int (integer) and long (long integer). However, Python has only int integer type after Python 3.x, python's numerical processing ability is quite strong, and basically, there is no limit on the number of bits.

As long as the hardware CPU can support it, even larger integers can be processed. Sometimes, for readability, we can use different numerical systems to represent integer values. For example, the memory address where data is stored is often expressed in hexadecimal. Integers contain positive or negative integers, which can be expressed in binary, hexadecimal or octal in addition to decimal, as long as 0b, 0x, and 0o are added before the numbers respectively to specify the binary system.

Refer to numbers with decimal points, that is, a real number in mathematics. In addition to the conventional representation method of the general decimal point, the scientific notation can also be used to represent it in an exponential form, such as 6e-2, where 6 is the significant number, and -2 is the exponent.

Numbers in computers are stored using IEEE 754 standard specification. Floating-point numbers in IEEE 754 standard cannot accurately represent decimals.

For example, num obtained from num = 0.1+0.2 is not equal to 0.3, but 0.30000000000000004. This is not a problem unique to Python. All programming languages have precision problems with floating-point numbers, so special care must be taken when performing floating-point numbers.

The following two decimal arithmetic methods are provided for readers' reference.

Decimal Module

This is a Python standard module library. Before using it, you need to import this module with import instruction before using it. After correctly importing this module, we can use the decimal. Decimal class to store accurate numbers. If the parameter is not an integer, we must pass in the parameter as a string.

For example:

import decimal

Num = decimal.decimal ("0.1")+decimal.decimal ("0.2")

And the result will be 0.3. Use the round () function to force the specified number of decimal places round(x[, n]) to be a built-in function, which returns the value closest to parameter x, and n is used to specify the number of decimal places returned.

For example:

result = 0.1+0.2

The program statement above print (round(num, 1)) takes the variable num to one decimal place, thus obtaining a result of 0.3. 2.2.3 Boolean Data Type (bool) is a data type that represents the logic and is a subclass of int, with only True value (true) and False value (false). Boolean data types are commonly used in program flow control. We can also use the value "1" or "0" to represent true or false values.

For example, the string and integer cannot be directly added, and the string must be converted to an integer. If all the operations are of numeric type, Python will automatically perform type conversion without specifying the forced conversion type.

For example:

num = 5+0.3

Result num=5.3 (floating-point number)

Python will automatically convert an integer to floating-point number for operation. In addition, Boolean values can also be calculated as numeric values. True means 1, False means 0.

For example:

num = 5+True

result num=6 (integer).

If you want to convert strings to Boolean values, you can convert them by bool function. Use the print () function in the following sample program to display Boolean values.

[sample procedure: bool.py]

converts bool type

print(bool(0))

print(bool(""))

```
print(bool(" ") )

print(bool(1) )
```

The execution results of the 05 print(bool("ABC ") sample program are shown. Program Code Resolution: Line 02: An empty string was passed in, so False was returned. Line 03 returns True because a string containing a space is passed in. When using Boolean, it values False and True, pay special attention to the capitalization of the first letter.

Constant

Constant refers to the value that the program cannot be changed during the whole execution process. For example, integer constants: 45, -36, 10005, 0, etc., or floating-point constants: 0.56, -0.003, 1.234E2, etc. Constants have fixed data types and values.

The biggest difference between variable and constant is that the content of the variable changes with the execution of the program, while the constant is fixed. Python's constant refers to the literal constant, which is the literal meaning of the constant. For example, 12 represents the integer 12. The literal constant is the value written directly into the Python program.

If literal constants are distinguished by data type, there will be different classifications, for example, 1234, 65, 963, and 0 are integer literal constants. The decimal value is the literal constant of the floating-point types, such as 3.14, 0.8467, and 744.084. As for the characters enclosed by single quotation marks (') or double quotation marks ("), they are all string literal constants. For example," Hello World "and" 0932545212 "are all string literal constants.

Formatting Input and Output Function

In the early stage of learning Python, the program execution results are usually output from the control panel or the data input by the user is obtained from the console. Before, we often use the print () function to output the program's execution results. This section will look at how to call the print () function for print format and how to call the input () function to input data.

The print format

The print () function supports the print format. There are two formatting methods that can be used, one is print format in the form of "%" and the other is print format in the form function. "%" print format formatted text can use "%s" to represent a string, "%d" to represent an integer, and "%f" to represent a floating-point number.

The syntax is as follows:

PRINT (formatted text (parameter 1, parameter 2, ..., parameter n))

For example:

score = 66

Print ("History Score: %d"% score")

Output

Result: History Score: 66

%d is formatted, representing the output integer format.

The print format can be used to control the position of the printout so that the output data can be arranged in order.

For example:

print("%5s history result: %5.2f"% ("Ram,"95))

The output results of the sample program

print("%5s history results: %5.2f"% ("Raj,"80.2))

The formatted text in the above example has two parameters, so the parameters must be enclosed in brackets, where %5s indicates the position of 5 characters when outputting, and when the actual output is less than 5 characters, a space character will be added to the left of the string.

%5.2f represents a floating-point number with 5 digits output, and the decimal point occupies 2 digits. The following example program outputs the number 100 in floating-point number, octal number, hexadecimal number and binary number format using the print function, respectively.

You can practice with this example program:

[Example Procedure: print_%.py]

Integer Output

visual = 100 in Different Decimal Numbers

print ("floating point number of number %s: %5.1f"% (visual,visual))

print ("octal of number %s: %o"% (visual,visual))

print ("hex of number %s: %x"% (visual,visual))

The execution result of the print ("binary of number %s: %s"% (visual,bin(visual))) will be displayed.

Program code analysis:

Lines 02-04: output in the format of floating-point number octal number and hexadecimal number.

Line 05: Since binary numbers do not have formatting symbols, decimal numbers can be converted into binary characters through the built-in function bin () and then output.

2. The output

Print format of the format () function can also be matched with the format () function. Compared with the% formatting method,

45

the format () function is more flexible. Its usage is as follows: print("{} is a hard-working student ... ."format ("First ranker ")).

Generally, the simple FORMAT usage will be replaced by the braces "{}," which means that the parameters in FORMAT () are used within {}. The format () function is quite flexible and has two major advantages: regardless of the parameter data type, it is always indicated by {}.

Multiple parameters can be used, the same parameter can be output multiple times, and the positions can be different.

For example: print("{0} this year is {1} years old ... ."format ("First ranker ,"18)), where {0} means to use the first parameter, {1} means to use the second parameter, and so on. If the number inside {} is omitted, it will be filled in sequentially.

We can also use the parameter name to replace the corresponding parameter, for example: print("{name} this year {age}.."format(name=" First ranker ,"age=18)) can specify the output format of the parameter by adding a colon":" directly after the number.

For example:

print('{0:.2f}'.format(5.5625)) means the first parameter takes 2 decimal places.

In addition, the string can be centered, left-aligned, or right-aligned with the "<" ">" symbol plus the field width.

For example:

print("{0:10}

score: {1: _ 10}." format ("Ram," 95))

print("{0:10}

results: {1:>10}."format("Raj," 87))

The output of the print("{0:10} result: {1:*<10}."format("Ram," 100)) program is shown. {1: _ 10} indicates that the output field width is 10, and the following line "_" is filled and centered. {1:>10} indicates that the output field is 10 wide and aligned to the right, and the unspecified padding characters will be filled with spaces. {1:*<10} indicates that the output field is 10 wide, filled with an asterisk "*" and aligned to the left.

Input Function:

Input() input is a common input instruction, which allows users to input data from "standard input device" (usually refers to keyboard) and transfer the numerical value, character or string entered by users to the specified variable. For example, if you calculate the total score of history and mathematics for each student, you can use the input command to let the user input the results of Chinese and mathematics, and then calculate the total score.

The syntax is as follows:

variable = input (prompt string) when data is Entered, and the enter key is pressed, the entered data will be assigned to the variable.

The "prompt string" in the above syntax is a prompt message informing the user to enter, for example, the user is expected to enter height, and the program then outputs the value of height.

The program code is as follows:

height =input ("Give exact your height:")

For example, score = input ("Give exact your math score:")

The output of the print("%s' math score: %5.2f"% ("ram,"float(score)))

When the program is executed, it will wait for the user to input data first when it encounters the input instruction. After the user completes the input and presses the Enter key, it will store the data input by the user into the variable score. The data input by the user is in string format. We can convert the input string into an integer, floating-point number, and bool type through built-in functions such as int (), float (), bool ().

The format specified in the example is floating point number (%5.2f), so call float () function to convert the input score value into floating point number. The next section will introduce more complete data type conversion. If we use an integrated

48

development environment such as Spyder, don't forget to switch the input cursor to Python console before inputting when the program is executed to input prompt information. Let's practice the use of input and output again through the sample program.

[Example Procedure: Format. Py] format.py】

name = input ("Give exact Name:")

che_grade = input ("Give a language score:")

math_grade = input ("Give Math Score:")

print("{0: 10} {1: > 6} {2: > 5}." format ("name," "language," "mathematics"))

The execution results of the 06print ("{0: < 10} {1: > 5} {2: > 7}." format (name, che _ grade, math _ grade)).

Program Code Analysis:

Lines 01-03: Require users to enter their names, Chinese scores, and math scores in sequence.

Lines 05 and 06: output the names, Chinese and math headers in sequence, and then output the names and results of the two subjects in the next line.

Data type conversion requires operations between different types in expressions. We can convert data types "temporarily," that is, data types must be forced to be converted.

There are three built-in functions in Python that cast data types.

1. int ():

Cast to integer data type

For example: x = "5"

num = 5 + int(x)

Print(dude) # Result: The value of 10 variable x is "5" and is of string type, so int(x) is called first to convert to integer type.

2. float ():

Cast to floating point data type

For example: x = "5.3"

dude = 5 + float(x)

Print(dude) # Result: The value of 10.3 variable X is "5.3" and is of string type, so float(x) is first used to convert to floating point type.

3. str ():

Cast to string data type

For example: first = "5.3"

dude = 5 + float(first)

Print ("The output value is"+str(dude)) # Result:

The output value is 10.3.

In the above program statement, the string of words "the output value is" in the print () function is a string type, the "+"sign can add two strings, and the variable dude is a floating point type, so the str () function must be called first to convert it into a string.

[sample procedure: conversion.py]

data type conversion

str = "{1}+{0} = {2}"

first = 150

second = "60"

The execution result of 04 print(str.format(first, second, first+int(second))) program

Line 01:

Since B is a string, specify its display format first. Note that the numerical numbering sequence of braces' {}' is {1}, {0}, {2}, so the display sequence of variables A and B is different from the parameter sequence in Format.

Line 04:

First, call int () to convert b to an integer type, and then calculate.

Hands-on Practice Exercise

-The pocket money bookkeeping butler designed a Python program that can input the pocket money spent seven days a week and output the pocket money spent every day. The sample program illustrates that this program requires the user name to be entered, and then the sum of spending for each day of the week can be entered continuously, and the pocket money spent for each day can be output.

Program code shows that the following is the complete program code of this example program.

[example program: money.py]

pocket money bookkeeping assistant

```
# -*- coding: utf-8 -*-
"""
```

You can enter pocket money spent 7 days a week and output the pocket money spent every day.

```
"""

name = value ("Give name:")
```

working1 = value ("Give the total amount of pocket money for the first working:")

working2 = value ("Give the total amount of pocket money for the next working:")

working3 = value ("Give the total amount of pocket money for the third working:")

working4 = value ("Give the total amount of pocket money for the fourth working:")

working5 = value ("Give the total spending of pocket money for the fifth working:")

working6 = value ("Give the total spending of pocket money for the sixth working:")

working7 = input ("Give the total allowance for the seventh working:")


```
print("{0:<8}{1:^5}{2:^5}{3:^5}{4:^5}{5:^5}{6:^5}{7:^5}." \

format("name,""working1,""working2,""working3," \

"working4,""working5,""working6," \

"working7"))
print("{0:<8}{1:^5}{2:^5}{3:^5}{4:^5}{5:^5}{6:^5}{7:^5}." \


format(name,working1,working2,working3,working4,working5,
working6,working7))
```

```
ave=total/7
```

print("total cost: {0:<8} average daily cost {1: 5}." format (total, ave))

With this, we have completed a brief explanation regarding python and its basic concepts that are necessary for understanding traditional programming methodology. In the next chapter, we will discuss in detail about Operators and other moderate level topics that are necessary for a clear understanding of programming.

Chapter 3: Operators in Python

In this chapter, we will explain about operators in detail. Operators are very necessary for programming knowledge. We will look at about them in detail in the next sections that follow.

Why are Operators Necessary?

One of the main characteristics of a computer is that it has strong computing power. It inputs the data obtained from the outside into the computer, carries out operations through programs, and finally outputs the desired results. In this chapter, we will discuss various types and functions of operators in Python and how to use Python to design expressions for arithmetic calculation and logical judgment.

No matter how complex the program is, the ultimate goal is to help us complete all kinds of operations, and the process must rely on one expression to complete. The expression is just like the usual mathematical formula,

For example: first=(second+third)*(first+10)/3.

The above mathematical formula is an expression; the $=,+,*$ and/sign are operators, and variables first, second, three, and constants 10 and 3 are operands. An expression consists of an operator and an operand.

What are Operands and Operators?

From the following simple expression (which is also a program statement): first = second+5 the above expression contains three operands first, second, and 5, an assignment operator "=," and an addition operator "+." In addition to arithmetic operators, Python also has comparison operators and logical operators applied to conditional judgment expressions.

In addition, there is an assignment operator that assigns the result of the operation to a variable. Operator if there is only one operand, it is called "unary operator," such as "-23" which expresses negative value. When there are two operands, they are called "binary operators." Arithmetic operators such as addition, subtraction, multiplication, and division are called "binary operators," such as 3+7. These various and fully functional operators have different operation priorities. This chapter will introduce the usage of these operators in detail.

Arithmetic operator

This is the most frequently used operator in programming languages. It is commonly used for some four operations, such as addition operator, subtraction operator, multiplication operator, division operator, remainder operator, division operator, exponent operator, etc. The +, -, *, and/operators are the same as our common mathematical operation methods, while the sign operator is mainly used to represent the positive/negative value of operands.

Usually, the + sign can be omitted when the constant is set to a positive number.

For example, "first=5" and "first=+5" have the same meaning. In particular, we should remind everyone that negative numbers are also represented by the "-" operator. When negative numbers participate in subtraction, in order to avoid confusion with subtraction operators, it is better to separate negative numbers with small brackets "()."

"/"and "//"are both division operators. The operation result of "/"is a floating-point number. The "//"will remove the decimal part of the division calculation result and only takes the integer. The "%" operator is the remainder.

For example:

first= 5

second= 2

Print(first/second) # result is floating-point number 2.5

Print(first// second) # result is integer 2

Print(first% second) # Result Is Remainder 1

If the result of the operation is not assigned to other variables, the data type of the operation result will be dominated by the variable whose data type occupies the largest memory space in the operand. In addition, when the operands are integers, and the operation result will produce decimals, Python will automatically output the result as decimals. We do not need to worry about the conversion of data types.

However, if the operation result is to be assigned to a variable, the memory space occupied by the variable must be large enough to prevent the excessively long part of the operation result data from being discarded. For example, if the result of the operation is a floating-point number and is assigned to an integer variable, the decimal part of the operation result will be truncated.

The division "/"operator in the arithmetic operator is a conventional division. The quotient obtained after the operation is a floating-point number. If the quotient is expressed as an integer, the int () function can be called.

Int(15/7) # Output 2 "* *" is a power operation, for example, to calculate the fourth power of 2:

print(7** 4) # The result is 28

Note that the priority of arithmetic operators +, -, *, and/is "multiply and divide first, then add and subtract." The following example illustrates that the operation result of the above formula of 10+2*3 is 16. In the expression, the precedence of parentheses is higher than in multiplication and division.

If the above expression is changed to (10+2)*3, the operation result will be 36. If operators with the same priority are encountered, the operations are performed from left to right. Let's take a look at the application of the simple four operations with an example program.

This sample program allows users to input Celsius temperature and convert it to Fahrenheit temperature through program operation.

The formula for converting Celsius temperature to Fahrenheit temperature is

F=(9/5)*C+32.

[sample procedure: sampletemp.py]

Celsius temperature is converted to Fahrenheit temperature

-*- coding: utf-8 -*-

#converts the input Celsius temperature into Fahrenheit temperature

Tip: F = (9/5) * C+32

Celsius = float(input ("Give the Celsius temperature"))

Fahren = (9 / 5) * Celsius + 32

The execution results of the 08 print ("Celsius temperature {0} is converted to Fahrenheit temperature {1}."format(C,F)) .

Program Code Resolution:

Line 02: Let the user input Celsius temperature and call float () function to convert the input into a floating-point data type.

Line 03: Converts the input Celsius temperature to Fahrenheit.

Line 04: Output the conversion between Celsius and Fahrenheit according to the specified format string. Incidentally, the "+" sign can be used to connect two strings.

sample="mno"+"pqrs"

result sample = "mnopqrs"

Assignment operator

The assignment operator "=" consists of at least two operands. Its function is to assign the value to the right of "=" to the variable to the left of the equal sign. Most beginners of many programming languages cannot understand the meaning of the equal sign "=" in programming languages.

It is easy to confuse it with the mathematical equivalent function. In programming languages, the "=" sign is mainly used for assignment, but we understand it from a mathematical point of view, and "=" used to be considered as the concept of "equal."

For example, the following program statement:

addition = 0;

addition= addition + 1;

The meaning of addition=0 in the above program statement is also easy to understand, but for the statement addition=addition+1, many beginners often cannot understand the meaning of this statement. In fact, the "=" in Python programming language is mainly used for "assignment."

We can imagine that when a variable is declared, the memory will be allocated, and the memory address will be arranged. Only when the specific value is set to the variable by using the assignment operator "=" will the memory space corresponding to the memory address be allowed to store the specific value.

In other words, addition= addition+1 can be seen as the result of adding 1 to the original data value stored in the sum memory address, and then re-assigning to the memory space corresponding to the sum memory address. The right side of the assignment operator "=" can be a constant, variable or expression, and will eventually assign the value to the variable on the left.

On the left side of the operator can only be variables, not numeric values, functions, expressions, etc. For example, the expression first-second=Third is an illegal program statement.

Python assignment operators have two types of assignment: single assignment and compound assignment.

1. Single assignment assigns the value on the right side of the assignment operator "=" to the variable on the left.

For example, the sample1 = 10 assignment operator can assign the same value to multiple variables at the same time, in addition to assigning one value to the variable at a time. If we want multiple variables to have the same variable value at the same time, we can assign variable values together. For example, if you want variables first, second, and third to have values of 100, the assignment statement can be written as follows:

first= second = third = 100 when you want to assign values to multiple variables in the same line of program statements, you can separate variables with ","." For example, if you want the variable first to have a value of 10, the variable second to have a value of 20, and the variable third to have a value of 30, write the assignment statement as follows: first, second, third = 10, 20, and 30 python also allows ";."

To continuously write several different program statements to separate different expressions.

For example, the following two lines of program code:

result= 10

Index = 12 ";"can be used. Write the above two lines on the same line.

Please look at the following demonstration:

result= 10;

Index = 12 # concatenates two program statements or expressions with semicolons in one line

2. The compound assignment

The compound assignment operator is formed by combining the assignment operator "=" with other operators. The prerequisite is that the source operand on the right side of "=" must have the same operand as the one receiving the assignment on the left side. If an expression contains multiple compound assignment operators, the operation process must start from the right side and proceed to the left side step by step,

For example:

first+= 1 # is equivalent to first = first+1

first-= 1 # is equivalent to first = first-1 with "A+=B;"

For example, a compound assignment statement is an assignment statement "first=first+second;" The simplified writing of is to perform the calculation of first+second first, and then assign the calculation result to the variable first.

In Python, first single equal sign "=" indicates assignment, and two consecutive equal signs "= =" are the "equality" of relational comparison operators and cannot be mixed. Note that when using the assignment operator, if you want to assign one variable to another, the first variable must first set the initial value; otherwise, an error will occur.

For example, result =result*10 because no initial value has been assigned to num variable, if the assignment operator is directly used, an error will occur because result variable has not been set to any initial value.

The following is a sample program for the comprehensive application of assignment operators.

[example program: assigning.py]

comprehensive application of assignment operator

01 # -*- coding: utf-8 -*-

02 """

03 Assignment application in python

```
04 """

05

06 black = 1

07 white = 2

08 red = 3

09

10 green = black+ white * red

11 print("{}.".format(black))

12 black += red

13 print("black={0}.".format (black, white)) #black=1+3=4

14 black -= white

15 print("black={0}.".format(black, white)) #black=4-2=2

16 black *= white

17 print("black={0}.".format(black,white)) #black=2*2=4

18 black **= white

19 print("black={0}.".format(black,white)) #black=4**2=16

20 black /= white

21 print("black={0}.".format(black,white)) #black=16/2=8
```

22 black //= white

23 print("black={0}."format(black,white)) #black=8//2=4

24 black %= red

25 print("black={0}."format(black,white)) #black=4%3=1

26 red = "Python"+"fun"

The execution result of the 27 print(s) program will appear.

Program code analysis:

Lines 12 and 13: assign the result of adding black and red to variable white, and then output the result value of black.

Lines 14 and 15: assign the result of subtraction between black and white to variable black, and then output the result value of black.

Lines 16 and 17: assign the result of multiplying black and white to variable black, and then output the result value of black.

Lines 18 and 19: assign the result of black and white power to variable black, and then output the result of black.

Lines 20 and 21: assign the result of dividing black and white to variable black, and then output the result value of black.

Lines 22 and 23: assign the result of dividing black and white integers to variable black, and then output the result value of black.

Lines 24 and 25: assign the remainder of black and white to variable black, and then output the result of black.

Comparison operator

The comparison operator is also called a relational operator and is used to determine whether the operands on the left and right sides of a conditional expression are equal, greater than or less than. When using relational operators, the results of the operations are either True or False, corresponding to Boolean values of true or false.

If the expression is True, it will get "true"; otherwise, it will get "False." The comparison operator can also be used in series, for example, black<white<=red equals black<red, and white<=red. Note that two consecutive equal signs "= =" are used to indicate the equality relationship, while a single equal sign "=" indicates the assignment operator.

As has been repeatedly stressed above, this gap is easy to cause negligence in writing program code. This is a very popular small "Bug" when debugging programs in the future.

[example program: comparisionsample.py]

Comprehensive application of comparison operator

```
01 # -*- coding: utf-8 -*-
02 """
03 Comparative Operator Practice
04 """
05 first = 56
06 second = 24
07 third = 38
08 primary = (first == second) # judge whether first equals second
09 secondary = (second! = third) # Judge whether second is not equal to third.
10 tertiary= (first >= third) # judge whether first is greater than or equal to third
11 print('is first equal to second: ',primary) # displays primary
12 print('second is not equal to third: ',secondary) # displays secondary
```

13 print ('whether first is greater than or equal to tertiary: ',tertiary) # displays tertiary.

Program Code Analysis:

Line 11:

first=56, second=24, which are not equal, so output False.

Line 12:

second=24, third=38, which are not equal, so the output is True.

Line 13:

first =56, third =38, first>third, so output True.

Logical operator

Logical Operator (LOGICAL OPERATOR) is used to judge basic logical operations and can control the process of program operation. Logical operators are often used in conjunction with relational operators, and the results of operations are only True and False. Logical operators include and, or, not, etc.

Beginners of programming use a truth table to observe logical operations more clearly. Truth table lists all combinations of operands true (T) and false (F) and the results of logical operations. As long as you understand the working principles of AND, or, and not, plus the aid of truth table, you can be familiar with logical operations quickly without memorizing it.

1. Logical and (And)

Logical AND must hold both left and right operands before the operation result is true. When either side is False, the execution result is false. For example, the logical result of the following instruction is true:

first= 10

second= 20

first < second and first ! = second #True Logical and Truth Table

2. Logical or (Or)

Logical OR As long as either of the left and right operands holds, the result of the operation is true. For example, the following logical operation is true:

sample = 10

result = 20

sample< result or sample == result #True if the expression sample < result on the left holds, the result of the operation is true, and there is no need to judge the relation comparison expression on the right.

3. Logical not (Not)

Logical not is a logical negation with slightly different usage. Only one operand can be operated. It is added to the left of the operand. When the operand is true, the NOT operation result is false. When the operand is false, the not result is true.

For example, the following logic operation result is true:

first= 10

second= 20

Not first<5 #True originally first<5 does not hold (the result is false), adding a not in front of it negates it, so the result is true.

Next, we use two simple statements to illustrate the use of logical operators:

value= 24

Result = (value% 6 == 0) and (value% 4 == 0) when using the and operator, result returns True because 24 is divisible by 6 and 4 at the same time.

Let's look at another example:

sum= 31

Value = Total% 3 = = or Total% 7 = = 0

When using the or operator, Value returns False because 31 cannot be divided exactly by 3 and 7. In addition, in Python programming language, when logical operations are performed using and or operators, the so-called "Short-Circuit" operation is used.

Let's take the and operator as an example to illustrate that the judging principle of short-circuit operation is that if the first operand returns True, the judgment of the second operation will continue, that is, if the first operand returns False, there is no need to judge further, which can speed up the execution of the program,

For example:

print (67>11) and (73>71)

The first operation result returns True.

In addition, if the short-circuit operation is applied to the or operator, the judgment of the second operand will only proceed when the first operand returns False. However, if the first operand returns True, there is no need to judge further, which can also speed up the execution of the program.

The following example program inputs the results of the two monthly exams and the final exam. As long as one of the monthly exams passes (more than 60 points), the final exam must pass so that the semester's results are considered as passing. Pass is output, otherwise FAIL is output.

[Example Procedure: coursePassOrFail.py]

Progress card python code

01 # -*- coding: utf-8 -*-

02 """

03 Enter the results of the two monthly exams and the final exam

04 Only one of the April exams passes, and the final exam passes

The result of the 2005 semester is considered as a PASS. Pass is output 05 PASS; otherwise, output FAIL

06 """

07 firstclass = int(input ("Give your primary monthly test score:"))

08 secondclass = int(input ("Give the result of the secondary monthly exam:"))

09 thirdclass = int(input ("Give the final exam result:"))

11 if (firstclass>=60 or secondclass>=60) and thirdclass>=60:

```
12- print("PASS")

13 else:

14 print("FAIL ")
```

Program Code Analysis:

The passing criteria for the title are the following two.

(1) "Only one passes the monthly exam": use logical or to judge.

(2) "Must pass the final exam": use logical and to judge. When an expression uses more than one logical operator, the priority of logical operators must be considered. Logical not will be evaluated first, followed by logical and, and finally logical or.

Two logical operators are used in the sample program: and and or. If the following formula is written directly, the logical AND will be executed first, and the semantics will become that the scores of the second monthly examination and the final examination must be greater than 60 points, and the result of execution will be incorrect. Primary> = 60 or secondclass > = 60 and thirdclass > = 60, so parentheses must be added to force the conditional expression to perform logical or judgment first.

For example, when the sample program is running, the first monthly test score is 90 points, the second monthly test score is 59 points, and the final test score is 80 points. You will get True, so the result will show PASS.

The data actually processed by the bit operator computer at the bottom layer are only 0 and 1, i.e., in binary form. Each bit of binary is also called a bit. Therefore, we can use a bitwise operator to perform logical operations between bits. Bit logic operators are especially used to calculate bit values in integers.

Four-bit logic operators are provided in Python language, namely &, |, and ~. 1.&(AND, bit logic AND operator). When performing AND operation, the corresponding two binary bits are both 1, so the operation result is 1; otherwise, it is 0. For example, if a=12 AND b=38, then a&b will get a result of 4 because the binary representation of 12 is 0000 1100 and the binary representation of 38 is 0010 0110. After performing and operation, the result will be 4 in decimal, as shown

(XOR, bit logic xor operator)

When performing xor operation, either of the corresponding two binary bits is 1(true), and the operation result is 1(true), but when both are 1(true) or 0(false), the result is 0(false).

For example, if first=12 and second=38, the result obtained by the first second is 42. As shown, when the or operation is performed by 3.| (OR), either of the corresponding two binary bits is 1, and the operation result is 1, that is, the result is 0 only when both bits are 0. For example, if first=12 and second=38, the result obtained by first | second is 46,

~ (not)

Not takes the complement of 1, i.e., all binary bits are inverted, i.e., 0 and 1 of all bits are exchanged. For example, first=12, the binary representation is 0000 1100, after the compliment is taken, since all bits of 0 and 1 will be exchanged, the calculated result is -13.

The so-called "compliment" means that when two numbers add up to a certain number (e.g., the decimal is 10), they are said to be complements of the certain number. For example, the 10's complement of 3 is 7, and the 10's complement of 7 is 3. For the binary system, there are two kinds of "1's complement system" and "2's complement system." 1's complement system "refers to the complement of two numbers that are 1 each other if the sum of the two numbers is 1, i.e., the complement of 0 and 1 that are 1 each other.

In other words, in order to obtain the complement of the binary number, one need only change 0 to 1 and 1 to 0. For example, $(1111101001010)2$ is complemented by $(10101010101)2$. "2's complement system" must calculate the 1's complement of the number in advance and add 1.

The following example program is an example of the application of bit operators.

[example program: bitwlseapplication.py]

Comprehensive application of bit operators

```
01 # -*- coding: utf-8 -*-
02 """
Comprehensive Application of 03-bit Operator
04 """
05 first = 12; second = 38
06 bin(first); Bin(second) # Call the bin () function to convert first and second into binary
07 print(first & second) # & operation result is 00000100, and then converted to decimal value
08 print (first second) operation is 10101010, which is then converted into a decimal value.
09 print(first | second) # | the result of the operation is 0101001010, which is then converted into a decimal value.
10 print(~first) # ~ operation is the execution result of the complement program taking
```

Program code analysis:

Line 07:

The binary representation of first=12 is first=00001100, the binary representation of second=38 is second=00100110, and the result of the &bit logic operation is 00000100, which is then converted into a decimal value of 4.

Line 08:

The binary representation of first=12 is first=00001100, the binary representation of second=38 is first = first=00100110, the result of bit logic operation is 00101010, and then the decimal value is 42.

Line 09:

The binary representation of first=12 is first =00001100, the binary representation of second=38 is first = 00100100110, and the result of | bit logic operation is 00101110, which is then converted to a decimal value of 46.

Line 10:

The binary representation of first=12 is first =00001100, and the result of its complement of 2 is 11110011, which is then converted to a decimal value of -13.

The bit shift operator

The bit shift operator shifts the binary bits of an integer value left or right by a specified number of bits. Python provides two-bit shift operators, as shown.

1) < < (left shift operator)

The left shift operator (< <) can shift the operand to the left by n bits. After the left shift, the bits beyond the storage range are discarded, and the bits left blank are supplemented by 0.

The syntax format is as follows: a<<n for example, the expression "12<<2," the binary value of the value 12 is 00001100, and after moving 2 bits to the left, it becomes 00110000, which is 48 decimal.

2) > > (right shift operator)

The right shift operator (> >) is the opposite of the left-shift operator, which can shift the operand content right by n bits and truncate the bits beyond the storage range after the right shift. Note the empty bit on the right at this moment. If the value is positive, fill 0 and negative, fill 1.

The syntax format is as follows: a>>n for example, the expression "12>>2," the binary value of the value 12 is 00001100, and after moving 2 bits to the right, it becomes 00000011, that is, 3 in decimal.

a=12 is declared in the program, allowing A and 38 to perform four kinds of bit logic operations and output the operation results. Finally, A is subjected to bit shift operations of left shift and right shift by two bits respectively and output the results.

[example program: bit shift.py]

Comprehensive application of bit operators

```
01 # -*- coding: utf-8 -*-
02 """
Comprehensive Application of 03-bit Operator
04 """
05
06 first=12
07 print ("%f&22.3 =% d"% (first, first&38)) # and operation
08 print ("%f | 22.3 =% d"% (first, first | 22.3)) # or operation
09 print ("%f 22.3 =% d"% (first, first 22.3)) # xor operation
10 print("~%f=%d"%(first,~first)) #NOT operation
11 print("%f<<2=%d" %(first,first<<2)) # shift left
12 print("%f>>2=%d" %(first,first>>2)) # the execution result of the right shift operation program
```

Operator Precedence

An expression often contains many operators. Operator precedence determines the sequence of program execution, which has a significant impact on the execution result and should not be taken lightly.

How to arrange the sequence of operators' execution?

At this time, the operation rules need to be established according to the priority. When an expression uses more than one operator, such as third=first+3*second, the priority of the operator must be considered. This expression will perform 3*second operation first, then add the operation result to first, and finally assign the added result to third. I remember when we were young in math class, the first formula we recited was "multiply and divide first, then add and subtract."

This is the basic concept of priority. When we encounter a Python expression, we first distinguish between operators and operands and then sort them out according to the priority of operators. For example, when there is more than one operator in an expression, the arithmetic operator is executed first, followed by the comparison operator, and finally, the logical operator.

The comparison operators have the same priority and are executed sequentially from left to right, while different arithmetic operators and logical operators have different priorities. The following are the priorities when calculating various operators in Python language.

Finally, consider the combination of operators from left to right, that is, operators with the same priority level will be processed from the leftmost operand. The parenthesis operator has the highest priority. The operation that needs to be executed first is added with the parenthesis "(). The expression in the parenthesis" () "will be executed first.

For example:

first = 100 * (90-30+45).

There are 5 operators in the expression above: =, *,-and+, and according to the operator priority rule, the operation in the parenthesis will be executed first with the priority of-,+,*, =.

[Example Program: operatorprecedence.py]

Comprehensive Application of Operator Priority

01 # -*- coding: utf-8 -*-

02 """

 Comprehensive Application of 03 Operator Priority

04 """

05 first = 2; second − 3

06 third = 9*(21/first + (9+first)/second)

07

08 print("first=," first)

09 print("second=," second)

The execution results of the print("9*(4/first +(9+first)/second)=," zthird) will be displayed.

Hands-on Practice Exercise

The report card statistics assistant is again time to practice. The theme is to make a report card statistics program. Enter the names of 10 students and their scores in mathematics, English, and Chinese. Calculate the total score and average score and judge which grade belongs to A, B, C, and D according to the average score. 3.8.1 The sample program shows that this time, the students' scores are not inputted one by one, which is too time-consuming.

The author has established the scores.csv file in advance. The file contains the names of 10 students and their scores in mathematics, English, and Chinese. The topic requirements for this exercise are as follows:

(1) Read in a CSV file with the file name scores.csv

(2) Calculate the total score, average score, and grade (A, B, C, D). A: an average of 80 to 100 points b: an average of 60 to 79 points c: an average of 50 to 59 points d: an average of fewer than 50 points

(3) Output the student's name, total score, average score (reserved to one decimal place) and grade. CSV file.

The so-called open data refers to data that can be freely used and distributed. Although some open data require users to identify the data source and the owner, most open platforms for government data can obtain the data free of charge. These open data will be published on the network in common open formats.

If different applications want to exchange data, they must use a common data format. CSV format is one of them. The full name is Comma-Separated Values. Fields are separated by commas and are all plain text files like TXT files. They can be edited by text editors such as Notepad. CSV format is commonly used in spreadsheets and databases.

For example, Excel files can export data to CSV format or import CSV files for editing. Much Open Data on the network will also provide users with directly downloaded CSV format data. When you learn how to process CSV files, you can use these data for more analysis and application.

Python Built-in CSV module can process CSV files very easily. CSV module is a standard library module, which must be imported with import instruction before use. Let's look at the usage of the CSV module. Usage of the CSV module can read CSV file or write to CSV file. Before reading, you must first open the CSV file and then use CSV.reader method to read the contents of the CSV file.

The code is as follows:

[get the module] csv # to load csv.py

With open ("furst.csv," encoding = "utf-8") ascsvfile:

open file specified as cssvfile

Reader = csv.reader (cssvfile)

returns reader object

For row in reader:

#for loop reads data row by row

Tips

If CSV files and. py files are placed in different folders, the full path of the files must be added. The open () command will open the csvfile and return the file object. The sample program assigns the file object to the CSV file variable. The default file uses unicode encoding.

If the file uses a different encoding, the encoding parameter must be used to set the encoding. The CSV file used in this sample program is in an utf-8 format without BOM, so encoding="utf-8." The csv.reader () function reads the CSV file, converts it into a reader object, and returns it to the caller. The reader object is a string List object that can be an iterator.

In the above program, the reader variable is used to receive the reader object, and then the data is read line by line through the

For loop: getit = csv.reader(csvfile)

 # returns the reader object

For row in reader:

#for loop reads data row by row into row variable list object is Python's Container Type.

Each element can be accessed by using the subscript (index, or index) of the bracketed "[]" collocation element. The subscript starts from 0 and is row[0] and ROW [1] from left to right, respectively. For example, to obtain the value of the 4th element, it can be expressed as follows: name = row[3] trick to open a file using with the statement before reading or writing the file, the file must be opened using the open () function.

When reading or writing is complete, the file must be closed using the close () function to ensure that the data has been correctly read or written to the file. If an exception occurs before calling the close () method, then the close () method will not be called.

For example:

f = open("results.csv") # to open the file

Csvfile = f.read() # read file contents

1 / 0 #error

F.close() # The program statement in line 3 of the close file made an error with denominator 0.

Once executed, the program will stop executing, so close () will not be called, which may risk file corruption or data loss. There are two special methods to avoid this problem: one method is to add try ... exception statements to catch errors, and the other method is to use with statements.

Python's with statement is equipped with a special method. After the file is opened, if the program is abnormal, the close () method will be automatically called, so as to ensure that the opened file is closed correctly and safely.

The program code shows that the scores.csv file used in this sample program contains the names of 10 students and their scores in mathematics, English, and Chinese. We need to sum up the scores in the three subjects, calculate the average score, and then use the average score to evaluate the grades.

The first line of the score CSV file is the title and must be skipped. Therefore, we use a variable x to record the currently read line number. The initial value of x is 0, and x must be greater than 0 before the if condition judgment expression is true. The code is as follows:

With open ("results. CSV," encoding = "utf-8") as CSV file:

first= 0 # sets the initial value of first to 0

For row in csv.reader(csvfile):

If first>0: # if first > 0, the if judgment expression is true

...

first+= 1 # is equivalent to indenting different blocks when writing Python programs with first=first+1. The above statement has three blocks, namely with...as block, for-loop block, and if block. The statement of first=0 must be placed outside the for loop, and the statement of first+= 1 must be placed inside the for loop, so that first will accumulate for each loop.

After entering the if block, the scores of the three subjects should be added up. Since the csv.reader function reads in string format, it must be converted into int format before calculation. Then assign the sum result to the variable score.

The score intervals of the four grades are as follows. firstclass: 80 ~ 100 points on average. secondclass: 60 ~ 79 points on average. thirdclass: average 50 ~ 59 points. fourthclass: below 50 on average. An average of 80 to 100 points is rated as "first" and so on, and 80 points are also in this interval. Therefore, the "> =" (greater than or equal to) relational operator must be used. If only average>80 is used to judge, 80 points will not fall in this interval.

The average score of 60 ~ 79 is rated as "second" and so on. This judgment requires two conditions, average>=60 and average<80, and both conditions must be met. Therefore, and must be used to judge: average > = 60 and average < 80. Since these two conditions are a numerical interval, the following expression can be written to indicate that the average value must be within 60 ~ 79. 60 <= average < 80 full if...else statement is as follows:

If average >= 80:

Grade = "first"

elif 60 <= average < 80:

Grade = "second"

elif 50 <= average < 60:

Grade = "third"

Else:

Grade = "Fail"

At last, you only need to output the scoreTotal, average, and grade with a print statement, and the execution result is displayed.

The following is the complete program code:

[sample procedure: Review_scores.py] transcript statistics assistant

01 # -*- coding: utf-8 -*-

02 """

03 Program Name: Report Card Assistant

04 Topic Requirements:

05 import CSV file

06 List the sum, average score and grade (first, second, third, fail)

07 first: average 80~100 points

08 second: average 60-79 points

09 third: average 50-59 points

10 fail: below 50 on average

```
11 """

12 import csv

14 print ("{0: < 3} {1: < 5} {2: < 4} {3: < 5} {4: < 5}." format
(",""name," "total score," "average score," "grade"))

15 with open("results.csv,"encoding="utf-8") as csvfile:

16 first = 0

17 for row in csv.reader(csvfile):

19 if first > 0:

20 scoreTotal = int(row[1]) + int(row[2]) + int(row[3])

21 indent = circle(scoreTotal / 3, 1)

23 if indent >= 80:

24 grade = "first"

25 elif 60 <= indent< 80:

26 grade = "second"

27 elif 50 <= indent < 60:

28 grade = "third"

29 else:

30 grade = "fail"
```

```
32          print("{0:<3}{1:<5}{2:<5}{3:<6}{4:<5}."format(first,
row[0], scoreTotal, average, grade))

34 result += 1
```

By this, we have completed a brief explanation about operators in detail. Operators are important to master programming languages because they can be used to create complex programs and software. The next chapter deals with various advanced programming concepts like loops and conditionals. We will discuss about these topics in detail. Why are you waiting? Let us explore the next chapters.

Chapter 4: Conditional and Loops in Python

This chapter describes moderate level topics like conditionals and loops in detail. We will use different examples to explain these topics in detail. Let us dive into knowing more about these concepts.

What is a sequence in Python?

The sequence of program execution is not a highway linking the north and the south. It can run all the way from the north to the south to the end. In fact, the sequence of program execution may be as complicated as a highway on the busy area, with nine turns and 18 turns, which is easy to make people dizzy.

In order to write a good program, it is very important to control the process of program execution. Therefore, it is necessary to use the process control structure of the program. Without them, it is absolutely impossible to use the program to complete any complicated work. In this chapter, we will discuss Python's various process control structures.

The programming language has been continuously developed for decades. Structured Programming has gradually become the mainstream of program development. Its main idea is to execute the entire program in sequence from top to bottom. Python language is mainly executed from top to bottom according to the sequence of program source code, but sometimes the execution sequence will be changed according to needs.

At this time, the computer can be told which sequence to execute the program preferentially through flow control instructions. The process control of the program is like designing a traffic direction extending in all directions for the highway system.

It is recognized that most program codes for process control are executed in sequence from top to bottom line after line, but for operations with high repeatability, it is not suitable to execute in sequence. Any Python program, no matter how complex its structure is, can be expressed or described using three basic control processes: sequence structure, selection structure, and loop structure.

The first line statement of the sequence structure program is the entry point and is executed from top to bottom to the last line statement of the program. The selection structure allows the program to select the program block to be executed according to whether the test condition is established or not. If the condition is True, some program statements are executed. If the condition is False, other program statements are executed.

In a colloquial way, if you encounter a situation A, perform operation A; if this is case b, operation b is executed. Just like when we drive to the intersection and see the signal lamp, the red light will stop, and the green light will pass. In addition, different destinations also have different directions, and you can choose the route according to different situations. In other words, the selection structure represents that the program will determine the "direction" of the program according to the specified conditions.

The function of loop flow control with loop structure is to repeatedly execute the program statements in a program block until the specific ending conditions are met. Python has a for loop and a while loop.

Selection Process Control

Selection Process Control is a conditional control statement that contains a conditional judgment expression (also referred to as conditional expression or conditional judgment expression for short). If the result of the conditional judgment expression is True (true), a program block is executed. If the result of the conditional judgment expression is false (True), another program block is executed.

The following describes the statements and their functions related to the selection process control in Python language.

If...Else Conditional Statement

If...else conditional statement is a fairly common and practical statement. If the conditional judgment expression is True (true, or represented by 1), the program statement in the if program block is executed. If the conditional judgment expression is not true (False, or represented by 0), the program statement in the else program block is executed. If there are multiple judgments, elif instruction can be added.

The syntax of the if conditional statement is as follows:

If conditional judgment expression:

If the conditional judgment expression holds, execute the program statement in this program block

Else :

If the condition does not hold, execute the program statement in this program block. If we want to judge whether the value of variable a is greater than or equal to the value of variable b, the condition judgment expression can be written as follows:

If a >= b:

If A is greater than or equal to B, execute the program statement in this program block

Else :

If a "no" is greater than or equal to b, the program statement if ... if...else conditional statement in this program block is executed.

In the use of the if ... else conditional statement, if the condition is not satisfied, there is no need to execute any program statement, and the else part can be omitted:

If conditional judgment expression:

If the condition is satisfied, execute the program statements in this program block. In addition, if the if ... if...else conditional statement uses logical operators such as and or, it is suggested to add parentheses to distinguish the execution order so as to improve the readability of the program,

For example: if (a==c) and (a>b):

If A equals C and A is greater than B, execute the program statement in this program block

Else :

If the above condition does not hold, the program statement in this program block is executed.

In addition, Python language provides a more concise conditional expression of if...else in the following format: X if C else Y returns one of the two expressions according to the conditional judgment expression. In the above expression, X is returned when C is true; otherwise, Y is returned.

For example, to determine whether the integer x is odd or even, the original program would be written as follows:

If (first % 2)==0:

second= "even number"

Else:

second= "odd number"

If print('{0}'.format(second)) is changed to a concise form, only a single line of program statements is required to achieve the same purpose.

The statements are as follows:

print('{0}'.format ("even" if (first% 2)==0 else "odd"))

If the if condition determines that the expression is true, it returns "even"; otherwise, it returns "odd." In the following sample program, we will practice the use of the if ... if...else statement. The purpose of the sample program is to make a simple leap year judgment program.

Let the user enter the year (4-digit integer year), and the program will determine whether it is a leap year. One of the following two conditions is a leap year: (1) leap every 4 years (divisible by 4) but not every 100 years (divisible by 100).

(2) leap every 400 years (divisible by 400).

[example procedure: leapYear.py]

judge whether it is a leap year

01 # -*- coding: utf-8 -*-

02 """

03 program name: leap year judging program

04 Topic Requirements:

05 Enter the year (4-digit integer year) to determine whether it is a leap year

06 condition 1. Every 4 leap (divisible by 4) and every 100 leap (divisible by 100)

07 condition 2. Every 400 leap (divisible by 400)

08 One of the two conditions met is a leap year.

09 """

10 year = int(input ("Give year:"))

12 if (year % 4 == 0 and year % 100 ! = 0) or (year % 400 == 0):

13 print("{0} is a leap year ."format(year))

14 Else:

The execution results of the

15 print("{0} is the year of peace ."format(year))

Program Code Resolution:

Line 10: Enter a year, but remember to call the int () function to convert it to an integer type.

Line 12-15: Judge whether it is a leap year.

Condition 1: every 4 leaps (divisible by 4) and every 100 leaps (not divisible by 100).

Condition 2: every 400 leaps (divisible by 400). One of the two conditions is a leap year. Readers are asked to inquire whether the following years are leap years: 1900 (flat year), 1996 (leap year), 2004 (leap year), 2017 (flat year), 2400 (leap year).

Multiple Choices

If there is more than one conditional judgment expression, elif conditional statement can be added. Elif is like the abbreviation of "else If." Although using multiple if conditional statements can solve the problem of executing different program blocks under various conditions, it is still not simple enough. Then, elif conditional statement can be used, and the readability of the program can be improved.

Note that if the statement is a logical "necessity" in our program. Elif and else do not necessarily follow, so there are three situations: if, if/else, if/elif/else.

The format is as follows:

If condition judgment

Expression 1:

If the conditional judgment expression 1 holds, the program statement in this program block is executed

Elif condition judgment

Expression 2:

If the conditional judgment expression 2 holds, execute the program statement in this program block

Else :

If none of the above conditions hold, execute the program statement in this program block,

For example:

If first==second:

If first equals second, execute the program statement in this program block

Elif first>b :

If first is greater than second, execute the program statement in this program block

Else :

if first is not equal to second and first is less than second, execute the program statement in this program block. The following example program is used to practice the use of IF multiple selection. The purpose of the sample program is to detect the current time to decide which greeting to use.

[sample procedure: currentTime.py]

Detects the current time to decide which greeting

01 # -*- coding: utf-8 -*-

02 """

03 Program Name: Detect the current time to decide which greeting to use

04 Topic Requirements:

05 Judging from the current time (24-hour system)

06 5~10:59, output "good morning"

07 11~17:59, output "good afternoon"

08 18~4:59, output "good night"

09 """

11 import time

13 print ("current time: {}." format (time.strftime ("%h:% m:% s"))

14 h = int(time.strftime("%H"))

16 if h>5 and h < 11:

17 print ("good morning!")

18 elif h >= 11 and h<18:

19 print ("good afternoon!")

20 else:

21 print ("good night!")

The execution results of the program will be shown on the screen.

The output shows the current time in the sample program to judge whether it is morning, afternoon, or evening, and then displays the appropriate greeting. Python's time module provides various functions related to time. The Time module is a module in Python's standard module library.

Before using it, you need to use the import instruction to import and then call the strftime function to format the time into the format we want. For example, the following program statement is used to obtain the current time.

Import time

Time.strftime ("%h:% m:% s")

 # 18: 36: 16 (6:36:16 p.m. 24-hour)

Time. strftime ("%i:% m:% s")

06:36:16 (6: 36: 16 p.m. 12-hour system) format parameters to be set are enclosed in parentheses.

Pay attention to the case of format symbols. The following program statement is used to display the week, month, day, hour, minute, and second.

Print (time.strftime ("%a,% b% d% h:% m:% s")) execution results are as follows: Monday, sep17 15: 49: 29 4.2.3 nested if sometimes there is another layer of if conditional statement in the if conditional statement. This multi-layer selection structure is called nested if conditional statement.

Usually, when demonstrating the use of nested if conditional statements, it is more common to demonstrate multiple choices with numerical ranges or scores. In other words, different grades of certificates will be issued for different grades of achievements.

If it is more than 60 points, the first certificate of competency will be given, if it is more than 70 points, the second certificate of competency will be given, if it is more than 80 points, the third certificate of competency will be given, if it is more than 90 points, the fourth certificate of competency will be given, if it is more than 100 points, the all-round professional certificate of competency will be given.

Based on nested if statements, we can write the following program:

Available= int(input ("Give a score:")

If available >= 60:

Print ('First Certificate of Conformity')

If available >= 70:

Print ('Second Certificate of Conformity')

If available >= 80:

Print ('Third Certificate of Conformity')

If available >= 90:

Print ('Fourth Certificate of Conformity')

If getScore == 100:

Print ('All-round Professional Qualification Certificate') is actually an if statement that is explored layer by layer. We can use the if/elif statement to filter the multiple choices one by one according to conditional expression operation and select the matching condition (True) to execute the program statement in a program block.

The syntax is as follows:

If Conditional Expression 1:

The program block to be executed in accordance with conditional expression 1

Elif conditional expression 2:

The program block to be executed in accordance with conditional expression 2

Elif conditional expression n:

The program block to be executed according to the conditional expression n

Else:

If all the conditional expressions do not conform, this program block is executed. When the conditional expression 1 does not conform, the program block searches down to the finally conforming conditional expression.

The elif instruction is an abbreviation of else if. Elif statement can generate multiple statements according to the operation of a conditional expression, and its conditional expression must be followed by a colon, which indicates that the following program blocks meet this conditional expression and need to be indented.

The following example program is a typical example of the combined use of nested if and if/elif statements. This program uses if to determine which grade the query results belong to. In addition, another judgment has been added to the sample program. If the score integer value entered is not between 0 and 100, a prompt message of "input error, the number entered must be between 0 and 100" will be output.

Comprehensive use of nested if statements example:

01 # -*- coding: utf-8 -*-

02 """

03 Examples of Comprehensive Use of Nested if Statements

04 """

05 result = int(input ('Give final grade:')

06

07 # First Level if/else Statement: Judge whether the result entered is between 0 and 100

08 if result >= 0 and result <= 100:

09 # 2nd level if/elif/else statement

10 if result <60:

11 print('{0} below cannot obtain certificate of competency'. format(result))

12 elif result >= 60 and result <70:

13 print('{0} result is d'. format(result))

14 elif result >= 70 and result <80:

15 print('{0} result is c'. format(result))

16 elif result >= 80 and result <90:

17 print('{0} result is level b'. format(result))

18 else:

19 print('{0} result is grade a'. format(result))

20 else:

The execution results of the

21 print ('input error, input number must be between 0-100')

Program code analysis:

Lines 7-21: first-level if/else statement, used to judge whether the input result is between 0 and 100.

Lines 10-19: the second-level if/elif/else statement, which is used to judge which grade the inquired result belongs to.

In the next section, we will discuss loops one of the most important concepts.

The Loop Repeat Structure

This mainly refers to the loop control structure. A certain program statement is repeatedly executed according to the set conditions, and the loop will not jump out until the condition judgment is not established. In short, repetitive structures are used to design program blocks that need to be executed repeatedly, that is, to make program code conform to the spirit of structured design.

For example, if you want the computer to calculate the value of 1+2+3+4+...+10, you don't need us to accumulate from 1 to 10 in the program code, which is originally tedious and repetitive, and you can easily achieve the goal by using the loop control structure. Python contains a while loop and a for loop, and the related usage is described below.

While loop

If the number of loops to be executed is determined, then using the for loop statement is the best choice. However, the while loop is more suitable for certain cycles that cannot be determined. The while loop statement is similar to the for loop statement and belongs to the pre-test loop. The working mode of the pre-test loop is that the loop condition judgment expression must be checked at the beginning of the loop program block.

When the judgment expression result is true, the program statements in the loop block will be executed. We usually call the program statements in the loop block the loop body. While loop also uses a conditional expression to judge whether it is true or false to control the loop flow. When the conditional expression is true, the program statement in the loop will be executed. When the conditional expression is false, the program flow will jump out of the loop.

The format of the While loop statement is as follows:

While conditional expression:

If the conditional expression holds, the flow chart of executing the while loop statement in this program block.

The while loop must include the initial value of the control variable and the expression for increasing or decreasing. When writing the loop program, it must check whether the condition for leaving the loop exists. If the condition does not exist, the loop body will be continuously executed without stopping, resulting in "infinite loop," also called "dead loop."

The loop structure usually requires three conditions:

(1) The initial value of the loop variable.

(2) Cyclic conditional expression.

(3) Adjust the increase or decrease the value of cyclic variables.

For example, the following procedure:

first=1

While first < 10: # Loop Condition Expression

print(first)

first += 1 # adjusts the increase or decrease value of the loop variable.

When first is less than 10, the program statement in the while loop will be executed, and then first will be added with 1 until first is equal to 10. If the result of the conditional expression is False, it will jump out of the loop.

For loop

For loop, also known as count loop, is a loop form commonly used in programming. It can repeatedly execute a fixed number of loops. If the number of loop executions required is known to be fixed when designing the program, then the for-loop statement is the best choice. The for loop in Python language can be used to traverse elements or table items of any sequence. The sequence can be tuples, lists or strings, which are executed in sequence.

The syntax is as follows:

For element variable in sequence:

Executed instructions

Else:

The program block of #else can be added or not added, that is, when using the for loop, the else statement can be added or not added. The meaning represented by the above Python syntax is that the for loop traverses all elements in a sequence, such as a string or a list, in the order of the elements in the current sequence (item, or table item).

For example, the following x variable values can all be used as traversal sequence elements of a

For loop:

first= "abcdefghijklmnopqrstuvwxyz "

second= ['january', 'march', 'may', 'july', 'august',

'october', 'december']

result= [a, e, 3, 4, 5, j, 7, 8, 9, 10]

In addition, if you want to calculate the number of times a loop is executed, you must set the initial value of the loop, the ending condition, and the increase or decrease value of the loop variable for each loop executed in the for-loop control statement. For loop every round, if the increase or decrease value is not specifically specified, it will automatically accumulate 1 until the condition is met.

For example, the following statement is a tuple (11 ~ 15) and uses the for loop to print out the numeric elements in the tuple: x = [11, 12, 13, 14, 15]

For first in x:

A more efficient way to write tuples is to call the range () function directly. The format of the range () function is as follows: range([initial value], final value [,increase or decrease value]) tuples start from "initial value" to the previous number of "final value." If no initial value is specified, the default value is 0; if no increase or decrease value is specified, the default increment is 1.

An example of calling the range () function is as follows: range (3) means that starting from the subscript value of 0, 3 elements are output, i.e., 0, 1 and 2 are three elements in total.

Range(1,6) means starting from subscript value 1 and ending before subscript value 6-1, that is, subscript number 6 is not included, i.e., 1, 2, 3, 4 and 5 are five elements. ·range (4,10,2) means starting from subscript value 4 and ending before subscript number 10, that is, subscript number 10 is excluded, and the increment value is 2, i.e., 4, 6 and 8 are three elements. The following program code demonstrates the use of the range () function in a for loop to output even numbers between 2 and 11 for i in range (2, 11, 2).

One more thing to pay special attention to when using the for loop is the print () function. If the print () is indented, it means that the operation to be executed in the for loop will be output according to the number of times the loop is executed. If there is no indentation, it means it is not in the for loop, and only the final result will be output.

We know that calling the range () function with the for loop can not only carry out accumulation operations but also carry out more varied accumulation operations with the parameters of the range () function. For example, add up all multiples of 5 within a certain range. The following sample program will demonstrate how to use the for loop to accumulate multiples of 5 within a range of numbers.

[Example Procedure: addition.py]

Accumulate multiples of 5 in a certain numerical range

```
01 # -*- coding: utf-8 -*-

02 """

03 Accumulate multiples of 5 within a certain numerical range

04 """

05 addition = 0 # stores the accumulated result

06

07 # enters for/in loop

08 for count in range(0, 21, 5):

09 addition += count # adds up the values

11 print('5 times cumulative result =',addition)

# Output cumulative result
```

Program code analysis:

Lines 08 and 09: Add up the numbers 5, 10, 15 and 20. In addition, when executing a for loop, if you want to know the subscript value of an element, you can call Python's built-in enumerate function. The syntax format of the call is as follows: for subscript value, element variable in enumerate (sequence element).

For example (refer to sample program enumerate. py):

names = ["ram," "raju," "ravi"]

for index, x in enumerate(names):

The execution result of the above statement in print ("{0}-{1}." format (index, x)) is displayed.

Nested loop

Next, we will introduce a for nested loop, that is, multiple for loop structures. In the nested for loop structure, the execution process must wait for the inner loop to complete before continuing to execute the outer loop layer by layer.

The double nested for loop structure format is as follows:

For example, a table can be easily completed using a double nested for loop. Let's take a look at how to use the double nested for loop to make the nine tables through the following sample program.

[Example Procedure: 99Table.py]

99 Table

01 # -*- coding: utf-8 -*-

02 """

03 Program Name: Table

04 """

05

06 for x in range(6,68):

07 for y in range(1, 9):

08 print("{0}*{1}={52: ^2}."format(y, x, x * y), end=" ")

99 is a very classic example of nested loops. If readers have learned other programming languages, I believe they will be amazed at the brevity of Python. From this example program, we can clearly understand how nested loops work. Hereinafter, the outer layer for the loop is referred to as the x loop, and the inner layer for loop is referred to as the y loop.

When entering the x loop, x=1. When the y loop is executed from 1 to 9, it will return to the x loop to continue execution. The print statement in the y loop will not wrap. The print () statement in the outer x loop will not wrap until the y loop is executed and leaves the y loop. After the execution is completed, the first row of nine tables will be obtained. When all X cycles are completed, the table is completed.

Note that the common mistake for beginners is that the sentences of the inner and outer loops are staggered. In the structure of multiple nested loops, the inner and outer loops cannot be staggered; otherwise, errors will be caused.

The continue instruction and break instruction are the two loop statements we introduced before. Under normal circumstances, the while loop is to judge the condition of the loop before entering the loop body. If the condition is not satisfied, it will leave the loop, while for loop ends the execution of the loop after all the specified elements are fetched. However, the loop can also be interrupted by continue or break. The main purpose of break instruction is to jump out of the current loop body, just like its English meaning, break means "interrupt."

If you want to leave the current loop body under the specified conditions in the loop body, you need to use the break instruction, whose function is to jump off the current for or while loop body and give the control of program execution to the next line of program statements outside the loop body. In other words, the break instruction is used to interrupt the execution of the current loop and jump directly out of the current loop.

Break

If a nested loop is encountered, the break instruction will only jump off the loop body of its own layer, and will be used together with the if statement,

For example:

For first in range (1, 10):

If first == 5:

Break

Print(first, end= "")

When first is equal to 5, the break statement will be executed to leave the for loop body, that is, the for loop will not continue to execute.

If we hope that a certain loop program can be executed continuously, and we will not leave the loop until a certain condition is met, we can use the break instruction at this time. If we want to design a game of guessing numbers, we require the user to enter a number between 1 and 100.

If the input is wrong, we will inform the user that the input number is too large or too small, and let the user repeat the input until the input number is exactly the same as the original default answer.

At this time, we can use the break command to jump off the loop and output the correct answer or the information such as the end of the game.

Look at the following program code:

number=9

while True:

```
Guess = int(input ('enter a number between 1 and 100->'))

if guess == number:

Print ('you guessed it, the number is:', number)

Break
```

Continue instruction

The function of the continue instruction is to force loop statements such as for or while to end the program currently executing in the loop and transfer control of program execution to the beginning of the next loop. In other words, if the continue instruction is encountered during the execution of the loop, the current round of loop will be immediately interrupted, all the program statements that have not yet been executed in the subsequent round of loop will be abandoned, and the program flow will be returned to the beginning of the while or for loop to start the next round of loop.

In contrast, the break instruction will end and jump off the current loop body, while the continue instruction will only end the current loop and will not jump off the current loop,

For example:

```
for first in range(1, 10):

if first == 5:
```

continue

When first is equal to 5, the continue instruction is executed, and the program will not continue to execute, so 5 is not printed by the print statement, and the for loop will continue to execute.

Practical Exercises

This section will use a sample program to review the above-mentioned related contents and make a simple password verification program. Example program shows that writing a Python program can allow users to enter passwords and perform simple password verification, but the number of entries is limited to three and login is not allowed if the current password is 5656.

1. Input Description

When entering for the first time, we can deliberately enter the wrong password, and the program will output "Wrong password!" and ask the user to enter the password again. We can try to enter the wrong password again, and we will also output "Wrong password!" If you enter the wrong password more than three times in a row, you will no longer be allowed to continue entering the password to log in, and you will be asked to enter "password error for three times, cancel login!" If the password entered in the input process is correct, the "correct password" will be output and ends the execution of the program.

Program Code Description

The complete program code is listed below. The default password for the password is the number 5656, and the variable I is used to record the total number of inputs. If the number of inputs exceeds three, it will jump out of the loop.

[sample procedure: password.py]

simple password verification procedure

01 # -*- coding: utf-8 -*-

02 """

03 let users enter passwords,

04 and perform simple password verification

05 However, the number of entries is limited to three. If the number exceeds three, login is not allowed.

06 If the current password is 5656.

07 """

08

09 password=5656 # uses the password variable to store passwords for verification.

10 first=1

```
12 while first<=3: # the number of inputs is limited to three

13 new_pw=int(input ("Give password:"))

14 if new_pw ! = password: # if the password entered is
different from the password

15 print ("wrong password! ! ! ")

16 first=first+1

17 continue # Jumps Back to while Start

18 else:

19 print ("correct password! ! ! ")

20 break

21 if first>3:

22 print ("password error 3 times, cancel login! ! ! \n");
```

Password Error Handling

With this, we have completed the moderate concepts like conditionals and loops that are very pivotal for the development of programs. In the next chapter, we will discuss modules and functions that are important for the application and software development. Python supports both function-oriented and object-oriented paradigms. We will discuss everything python offers for advanced programmers in detail in the next chapters.

Chapter 5: Modules and Functions in Python

This chapter will introduce the concepts of modules and functions in Python. Structured programming can decompose complex problems into several components and define and implement modules and functions for the components. This chapter will discuss in detail the features of Python modules and functions. Finally, Python's functional programming will be introduced.

Python Program Structure

Python's program consists of a package, a module, and functions. A module is a set that deals with a certain class of problems. A module consists of functions and classes. A package is a collection of modules.

A package is a toolbox for specific tasks. Python provides many useful toolkits, such as string processing, graphical user interface, Web application, graphical image processing, etc. Using these toolkits can improve the development efficiency of programmers, reduce the complexity of programming, and achieve the effect of code reuse.

These self-contained toolkits and modules are installed in the Lib subdirectory under Python's installation directory.

For example, for the xml folder in the Lib directory, an xml folder is a package that is used to complete XML application development. There are several sub-packages in the xml package: dom, sax, etree, and parsers. The file __init__.py is the registration file of the xml package, without which Python will not recognize the xml package. The xml package is defined in the system dictionary table available on internet websites.

Note that the package must contain at least one __init__.py file. The contents of the __init__.py file can be empty, which is used to identify the current folder as a package.

Modules are important concepts in Python. Python programs are composed of modules one by one. I've already touched on modules, and a Python file is a module. The following will introduce the concept and characteristics of the module.

Module Creation

A module organizes a set of related functions or codes into a file. A file is a module. Modules consist of code, functions, or classes. To create a file named myModule.py, a module named myModule is defined. Define a function func () and a class MyClass in the myModule module. A method myFunc () is defined in the MyClass class.

```
01 # custom module

02 def func():

03 print ("MyModule.func()")

04

05 class example:

06 def examplefun(self):

07 print ("MyModule.example.examplefun()")
```

Then create a file called _ myModule.py in the directory where mymodule.py resides. The functions and classes of the myModule module are called in this file.

```
01 # Calls Classes and Functions of Custom Modules

02 import myexample # import module

03

04 myexample.func()

05 myClass=myexample.MyClass()

06 myClass.myFunc()
```

[Code Description]

Line 2

Code Import Module myexample.

Line 4

This calls the examples' function. You need to prefix myexample when calling; otherwise, Python does not know the namespace where function() is located.

Output results:

myexample.func()

Line 5

This code creates an instance of the class Myexample. You also need to call the class with the prefix myexample.

Line 6

This calls the method myexample() of the class.

Output results:

myexample.Myexampleclass.myexample()

Note that myModule.py and call_myModule.py must be placed in the same directory or in the directory listed in sys.path; otherwise, Python interpreter cannot find the customized module.

When Python imports a module, Python first looks for the current path, then the lib directory, site-packages directory (Python\Lib\site-packages) and the directory set by the environment variable PYTHONPATH. If the imported module is not found, search the above path to see if it contains this module. You can search the module's search path through the sys.path statement.

Module Import

Before using a module's function or class, you must first import the module. The module import has been used many times before, and the module import uses the import statement.

The format of the module import statement is as follows.

import nameofthemodule

This statement can be directly imported into a module. When calling a function or class of a module, you need to prefix it with the module name in the following format.

nameofthemodule.func()

If you do not want to use prefixes in your program, you can import them using the from...import... statement. The format of the from...import... the statement is as follows.

from nameofthemodule import nameofthefunction

This compares the difference between the import statement and the from ... import ... statement. Importing all classes and functions under the module can use import statements in the following format.

from nameofthemodule import *

In addition, the same module file supports multiple import statements. For example, define a module named myexample. The module defines a global variable count and a function (). Every time the function () is called, the value of the variable count is incremented by 1.

01 number =1

02

03 def function ():

04 global number

05 number=number+1

06 return the number

Import myexample module several times to see the result of variable count.

01 import myexample

02 print("count =," myexample.func())

03 myexample.count=10

04 print ("count =," myexample.count)

05

06 import myexample

07 print ("count =," myexample.func())

[Code Description]

Line 1

Code Import Module myexample.

The second line of code calls the function () in the module. At this time, the value of the variable count is equal to 2.

Output result:

number=2.

The third line of code assigns a value to the variable count in the module myexample, where the value of the variable count is equal to 10.

The fourth line of code gets the value of the variable count.

Output result:

number=10.

The code in line 6 is imported into module myexample again, and the initial value of variable count is 10.

The seventh line of code calls function(), and the value of variable count is increased by 1.

Output result:

number =11.

Import statements in Python are more flexible than those in Java. Python's import statement can be placed anywhere in the program or even in conditional statements.

Add the following statement after the above code segment:

01 # import placed in the conditional statement

02 if myexample.number> 1:

03 myexample.number=1

04 else:

05 import myexample

06 print ("count =," myexample.number)

[Code Description]

The second line of code judges whether the value of myexample.number is greater than 1.

Line 3 code, if the value of count is greater than 1, set the value of variable count to 1. Since the value of the variable count in the preceding code segment is 11, the value of the variable count is assigned to 1.

Line 5 code, if the value of count is less than or equal to 1, import statement.

The sixth line of code outputs the value of the variable count. Output Result: count=1

Properties of Modules

Modules have some built-in attributes that are used to complete specific tasks, such as __name__, __doc__. Each module has a name; for example, __name__ is used to determine whether the current module is the entry of the program. If the current program is in use, __name__ has a value of "__main__." Usually, a conditional statement is added to each module to test the function of the module separately.

For example, create a module myexample.

01 if __name__ =='__main__':

02 print ('myexample runs as main program')

```
03 else:
```

```
04 print ('myexample Called by Another Module')
```

[Code Description]

The first line of code determines whether this module is running as the main program. Run the module myexample separately, and the output results are as follows. Myexample runs as the main program.

Create another module myexample. This module is very simple, just import module myexample.

```
01 import myexample
```

```
02 print (__doc__)
```

[Code Description]

Run the module myexample and output the result:

Myexample is called by another module. The second line of code calls another module attribute __doc__. Since the module does not define a document string, the output result is None.

Output Result:

None

Built-in Functions of Modules

Python provides an inline module build-in. The inline module defines some functions that are often used in development. These functions can be used to realize data type conversion, data calculation, sequence processing, and other functions.

The functions commonly used in inline modules will be described below.

1. apply()

The apply function has been removed from Python3, so it is no longer available. The function of calling the variable parameter list can only be realized by adding * before the list.

2. filter()

Filter () can filter a sequence to determine whether the result returned by the parameters of the custom function is true or not

Filter and return the processing results at one time.

The declaration of filter () is as follows.

class filter(object)

filter(function or None, iterable) --> filter object

The following code demonstrates the function of the filter () filter sequence.

Filters out numbers greater than 0 from a given list.

```
01 def func(x):
02 if first> 0:
03 return first
04
05 print (filter (function, range (-39,10))) # calls the filter function and returns the filter object
06 print (list (filter (function, range (-94,10)))) # converts filter object to list
```

[Code Description]

In line 5, use range () to generate the list to be processed, and then transfer the values of the list to func (). Func returns the result to filter () and finally returns the resulting yield as an iterable object, which can be traversed.

The output is as follows:

<filter object at 0x1022b2750>

Note that the parameter of the filter function func () in filter () cannot be empty. Otherwise, there is no variable that can store the sequence element, and func () cannot handle filtering.

3. reduce()

Continuous operations on elements in a sequence can be handled through loops. For example, to accumulate elements in a sequence. Python's reduce () can also implement continuous processing. In Python2, reduce () exists in global space and can be called directly. In Python3, it is moved to the functools module, so it needs to be introduced before use. The declaration of reduce () is as follows.

reduce(function, sequence[, initial]) -> result

[Code Description]

Parameter function is a self-defined function, which implements continuous operation of the parameter sequence in function function().Parameter initial can be omitted. If the initial is not empty, the value of initial will be passed into function() for calculation first. If the sequence is empty, the value of initial is processed.

The return value of reduce () is the calculated result of func ().

The following code implements the accumulation of numbers in a list.

01 def addition(first, second):

02 return first+second

```
03 form functools import reduce

# Introduce reduce

04 print (reduce(addition, range(0, 10)))

05 print (reduce(addition, range(0, 10), 10))

06 print (reduce(addition, range(0, 0), 10))
```

[Code Description]

The first line of code defines an addition () function, which provides two parameters and performs an accumulation operation.

Line 4 code, perform accumulation calculation on 0+1+2+3+4+5+6+7+8+9. The output is 45.

Line 5 code, perform accumulation calculation on 10+0+1+2+3+4+5+6+7+8+9. The output is 55.

In line 6, because range(0, 0) returns an empty list, the return result is 10.

The output is 10.

Reduce () can also perform complex cumulative calculations such as multiplication and factorial on numbers. Note that if you use reduce () for cumulative calculation, two parameters must be defined in sum to correspond to the operands on both sides of the addition operator.

4. map()

Map () is used to "unpack" tuple, and the first parameter of map () is set to None when calling. Map () is very powerful and can perform the same operation on each element of multiple sequences and return a map object. The declaration of map () is as follows.

class map(object)

map(func, *iterables) --> map object

[Code Description]

The parameter function is a custom function that implements the operation on each element of the sequence. The parameter iterables is a sequence to be processed, and the number of parameters iterables can be multiple.

The return value of map () is the processed list of sequence elements.

The following code implements the exponentiation of the numbers in the list.

01 def power(first): return first ** first

02 print (map (power, range (1,5))) # print map object

```
03 print (list (map (power, range (1,5))) # converted to list
output

04 def power2(first, second): return first ** second

05 print (map (power2, range (1,5), range (5,1,-1))) # print map
object

06 print (list (map (power2, range (1,5), range (5,1,-1))) #
converted to list output
```

[Code Description]

The first line of code defines a power () function, which implements the power operation of numbers.

The second line of code passes the numbers 1, 2, 3 and 4 into the function power, in turn, converts the calculation result yield into an iterable object, and outputs the result:

map object at 0x7675678>

The third line of code converts the map object into a list and prints it out, and outputs the result:

[1, 4, 27, 256]

The fourth line of code defines a power2 () function to calculate the Y power of X.

The fifth line of code provides two list parameters. 1 5, 2 4, 3 3 and 4 2 are calculated in turn, and the calculated results yield into an iterable object. Output results:

<map object at 0x19876543234560>

Line 6 converts the map object into a list output.

Output results:

[21, 16, 29, 26]

Note that if multiple sequences are provided in map (), the elements in each sequence are calculated one by one. If the length of each sequence is not the same, then the short sequence is supplemented with None before calculation.

Custom Packages

A package is one that contains at least __init__.py files . Folders Python package and Java package have the same function, both of which are to realize the reuse of programs. They combine the code that realizes a common function into a package and call the services provided by the package to realize reuse. For example, define a package parent. Create two sub-packages pack and pack2 in the parent package.

A module myModule is defined in the pack package, and a module myModule2 is defined in the pack2 package. Finally, define a module main in package parent and call sub-packages pack and pack2.

The __init__.py program for the package pack is as follows:

01 if __name__ =='__main__':

02 print ('run as first program')

03 else:

04 print ('pack initialization')

This code initializes the pack package and directly outputs a string. When the pack package is called by other modules, "pack initialization" will be output. The myexample module of the package pack is shown below.

01 def function():

02 print ("pack.myexample.func()")

03

04 if __name__ =='__main__':

05 print ('myexample runs as first program')

06 else:

07 print ('myexample Called by Another Module')

When pack2 is called by other modules, the __init__.py file will be executed first. The __init__.py program for pack2 is as follows.

```
01 if __name__ =='__main__':
02 print ('run as first program')
03 else:
04 print ('pack2 initialization')
```

The myModule2 modules of pack2 are as follows.

```
01 def func2():
02 print ("pack2.myexample2.func()")
03
04 if __name__ =='__main__':
05 print ('myexample2 runs as main program')
06 else:
07 print ('myexample2 called by another module')
```

The main module below calls the functions in pack and pack2 packages.

```
01 from pack import myexample
```

```
02 from pack2 import myexample2

03

04 myexample.func()

05 myexample2.func2()
```

[Code Description]

The first line of code imports the myexample module from the pack package. The myexample module is called by the main module, so the output string "myexample is called by another module."

The output is as follows:

Pack initialization

Myexample is called by another module. The second line of code imports the myexample2 module from the pack2 package.

The output is as follows:

Pack2 initialization

Myexample2 is called by another module. The fourth line of code calls function() of myexample module.

The output is as follows:

pack.myexample.func()

Line 5 calls func2 () of myexample2 module.

The output is as follows:

pack2.myexample2.function()

__init__.py can also be used to provide a list of modules for the current package. For example, add a line of code before the __init__.py file of the pack.

__all__=["myexample"]

__all__ is used to record the modules contained in the current pack. The contents in square brackets are the list of module names. If the number of modules exceeds 2, separate them with commas. Similarly, a similar line of code was added to the pack2 package.

__all__=["myexample2"]

In this way, all modules in pack and pack2 can be imported in the main module at one time.

The modified main module is as follows:

01 from pack import *

02 from pack2 import *

03 myexample.func()

05 myexample2.func2()

[Code Description]

Line 1 code, first execute the __init__.py file of the pack and then look for the modules contained in the pack in the __all__ attribute. If the __init__.py file of the pack does not use the __all__ attribute to record the module name, the main module will not recognize the myexample module when it is called.

Python will prompt the following error.

NameError: name 'myexample' is not defined.

Line 2 code has the same function as line 1 code.

Function

A function is a piece of code that can be called repeatedly and returns the desired result by entering the parameter value. The previous example has used Python's built-in functions many times and has also customized some functions. Python's functions have many new features, which will be described one by one below.

Definition of function

A function definition is very simple, using the keyword def definition. Functions must be defined before use, and the type of function is the type of return value. Python functions are defined in the following format.

01 def function name (parameter 1, parameter 2 ...):

02 ...

03 return expression

The function name can be a string of letters, numbers, or underscores, but cannot begin with a number. The parameters of the function are placed in a pair of parentheses. The number of parameters can be one or more. The parameters are separated by commas. Such parameters are called formal parameters.

The parenthesis ends with a colon, and the body of the function follows the colon. It uses a dictionary to implement a switch statement. Now wrap this code into a function. It involves three parameters: two operands and an operator.

The modified code is as follows.

01 # Function

02 from __future__ import division

03 def calculation (first, second, operator):

04 result={

05 "+":first+second,

06 "-":first-second,

07 "*":first * second,

```
08 "/":first / second

09 }
```

[Code Description]

The third line of code defines the function calculation(); the first and second are the two operands of the four operations, and the operator is the operator. The values of these three parameters are passed from the actual parameters.

Lines 4 to 9 are the main body of the function, realizing the operation of operands.

Call of function

```
01 # Function

02 print (calculation(1, 2, "+"))
```

[Code Description]

calculation () is written after the print statement and directly outputs the return value of the function. The output is "3."

Note that the actual parameters must correspond to the formal parameters one by one, otherwise erroneous calculations will occur — exceptions to parameters with default values.

Parameters of function

In C and C++, there are two ways to pass parameters: value passing and reference passing. Anything in Python is an object, so parameters only support the way references are passed. Python binds the value of the actual parameter to the name of the formal parameter through a name binding mechanism. That is, the formal parameter is passed to the local namespace where the function is located, and the formal parameter and the actual parameter point to the same storage space in memory In between.

The parameters of the function support default values. When a parameter does not pass an actual value, the function uses the default parameter calculation. For example, you can provide a default value for all parameters of calculation ().

Default Parameter for functions

01 # Function

02 def calculation(first=1, second=1, operator="+"):

03 result = {

04 "+" : first+second,

05 "-" : first-second,

06 "*" : first * second,

```
07 "/" : first / second

08 }

09 return result.get(operator)

# returns the calculation result

11 print (calculation(1, 2))

12 print (calculation(1, 2, "-"))

13 print (calculation(first=3, operator="-"))

14 print (calculation(second=4, operator="-"))

15 print (calculation(second=3, first=4, operator="-"))
```

[Code Description]

The code in line 2 defines the default value of the parameter by using an assignment expression.

In line 11, the values of parameters x and y are assigned to 1 and 2 respectively, and the default value "+" is used for parameter operator. The output is "3."

Line 12 provides 3 actual parameters, which will override the default values of formal parameters, respectively. The output result is "-1."

Line 13 code, specify the values of parameters y and operator. The output result is "-2." The parameters must be passed in the form of assignment expressions. Otherwise, the Python interpreter will mistakenly assume x=3, y="- ." Therefore, the following wording is wrong.

print(calculation(3, "-"))

Line 14 code, specify the values of parameters x and operator. The output is "3."

Line 15 code, using assignment expression to pass parameters, can reverse the order of the parameter list. The output is "1."

Parameters can be variables or built-in data structures such as tuples and lists.

01 # list is passed as a parameter

02 def calculation(args=[], operator="+"):

03 first = args[0]

04 second = args[1]

05 result = {

06 "+" : first+second,

07 "-" : first-second,

08 "*" : first * second,

```
09 "/" : first/ second

10 }

12 print(calculation([1, 2]))
```

[Code Description]

The second line of code combines the parameters x and y into one parameter and passes the values of x and y through the args list.

Lines 3 and 4 of code, take out parameter values from the list and assign them to variables x and y respectively. Line 12 code, pass the list [1,2] to calculation (). The output is "3."

Because parameters implement the mechanism of name binding, unexpected results may occur when using default parameters.

```
01 def join(args=[]):

02 args.join(0)

03 print (args)

04

05 join()

06 join([1])
```

07 join()

[Code Description]

The first line of code defines a join () function, and the argument is a default list.

The second line of code joins an element 0 to the list.

Line 5 calls join (), using the default list. The output is' [0]'.

Line 6 code, passed a list [1], join () is joined with an element 0. The output is "[1, 0]."

The seventh line of code calls join () again, and the list used at this time is args called for the first time, so args will add another element 0 on the original basis.

The output is' [0, 0]'.

To avoid this problem, a conditional judgment statement can be added to join (). If there are no elements in the list args, empty the args list before adding elements.

01 def join(args=[]):

02 if len(args) <=0:

03 args=[]

04 args.join(0)

05 print (args)

06

07 join()

08 join([1])

09 join()

[Code Description]

The second line of code uses len () to determine whether the length of the list args is greater than 0. If less than or equal to 0, args is set to an empty list, i.e., function parameters are unbound.

Line 4 adds an element 0 to the list.

Line 7 calls join (), using the default list. The output is' [0]'.

In line 8, a list [1] is passed, and an element 0 is joined to join (). The output is "[1, 0]."

The 9th line of code calls join (), which cancels the name binding of the parameter through the judgment of len(args). The output is' [0]'. In development, it is often necessary to pass variable-length parameters.

This requirement can be met by using the identifier "*" before the parameter of the function. "*" can refer to tuples and combine multiple parameters into one tuple.

01 # Pass Variable Parameters

02 def function(*args):

03 print args

04 function(1, 2, 3)

[Code Description]

Line 2 code, use identifier "*" before argument args.

The code in line 3 outputs the value of the parameter. Because the parameter uses the form of "*args," the actual parameter passed in is "packed" into a tuple, and the output result is "(1, 2, 3)."

The fourth line of code calls the function func (). The parameters "1," "2" and "3" become elements of args tuples.

Python also provides another identifier "* *." Add "* *" before the formal parameter to refer to a dictionary and generate the dictionary according to the assignment expression of the actual parameter. For example, the following code implements matching tuple elements in a dictionary.

When defining a function, two parameters are designed: one is the tuple to be matched, which is denoted as "* t"; the other is a dictionary, which means "*d." When the function is called, the actual parameters are divided into two parts: one part is several numbers or strings, and the other part is assignment expression.

```
01 # Pass Variable Parameters

02 def find(*one, **two):

03 keys = one.keys()

04 values = two.values()

05 print(keys)

06 print (values)

07 for arg in t:

08 for key in keys:

09 if arg == key:

10 print ("find:,"d[key])

12 find("one," "three," one="1,"two="2,"three="3")
```

[Code Description]

"*t" in line 2 corresponds to "one" and "three" in line 12. "One" and "three" form a tuple t. "**d" corresponds to "one="1," two="2," three="3"," generating a dictionary {one: "1,"two:"2,"three: "3"}.

Line 5 code output results:

['three', 'two', 'one']

Line 6 code output results:

['3', '2', '1']

Lines 7 to 10 look up the value in tuple t in dictionary d. If found, output.

find: 1

find: 3

Note that "*" must be written before "* *," which is a grammatical rule.

Return value of function

The return of a function uses a return statement, which can be followed by a variable or expression. Let's perfect calculation () and add a return statement.

The code is as follows:

01 from __future__ import division

02 def calculation(first, second, operator):

```
03 result={

04 "+":first+second,

05 "-":first-second,

06 "*":first * second,

07 "/":first / second

08 }

09 return result.get(operator)

# returns the calculation result
```

[Code Description]

Line 9 calls the dictionary's get (), obtains the corresponding expression, and returns the calculated result.

For C and Java, if the function body is not returned by return statement, but the function is called in the assignment statement, the program will have errors after compilation. Python does not have this syntax restriction. Even if a function does not return a value, it can still get the return value.

For example:

```
01 # function without return statement returns None

02 def function():
```

```
03 pass

04

05 print (function())
```

[Code Description]

The second line of code defines a function (), the main body of the function does not have any implementation code, and pass keyword is equivalent to a placeholder.

The fifth line of code outputs the return value of function (). Because there is no return statement, the return value is None. The output is "None."

None is an object in Python and does not belong to numbers or strings. When the return statement in the function does not take any parameters, the returned result is also None.

```
01 def function ():

02 return

03

04 print (function ())
```

If you need to return multiple values, you can "package" these values into tuples. When calling, unpack the returned tuple. The following code implements the inversion of input variables.

For example, enter 0, 1, and 2 and return 2, 1, and 0.

```
01 # return returns multiple values

02 def function(first, second, third):

03 l=[first, second, third]

04 l.reverse()

05 numbers=tuple(l)

06 return numbers

07

08 first, second, third=func(0, 1, 2)

09 print (first, second, third)
```

[Code Description]

The second line of code defines a function (), which returns the 3 values after inverting the 3 parameters passed in. The third line of code "packages" the three parameters into a list. Line 4 code inversion list. The fifth line of code loads the list into a tuple. The sixth line of code returns tuples, that is, 3 numbers.

The 8th line of code calls function () to obtain the returned tuple and "unpack" it into 3 variables. The ninth line of code outputs the values of the three variables.

A slight improvement in the code can also lead to a second solution.

```
01 def function(one, two, three):
02 l=[one, two, three]
03 l.reverse()
04 one, two, three=tuple(l)
05 return one, two, three
06
07 one, two, three =function(0, 1, 2)
08 print (one, two, three)
```

[Code Description]

The fourth line of code "unpacks" tuples and assigns the inverted values to variables A, B and C respectively. In line 5, you can return multiple values with comma-separated expressions after the return.

Line 7 calls func (), assigning a, b and c to x, y and z respectively.

You can use more than one return statement in a function. For example, in each branch of the if ... else ... statement, different results are returned.

Multiple return Statements

```
02 def function(one):
03 if one> 0:
04 return "one> 0"
05 elif one ==0:
06 return "one ==0"
07 else:
08 return "one<0"
09
10 print (function(-2))
```

[Code Description]

Return "one> 0" when the passed-in parameter is greater than 0. When the passed-in parameter is equal to 0, "one = = 0" is returned. When the passed-in parameter is less than 0, return "one<0."

Note that multiple return statements are not recommended. Too many return statements often complicate the program, so the code needs to be refactored.

If there is more than one return statement in the program, you can reduce the return statement by adding a variable.

Reconstruction of function

```
01 # Multiple return Statements

02 def function(one):

03 if one> 0:

04 result="one> 0"

05 elif one ==0:

06 result="one ==0"

07 else:

08 result="one<0"

09 return result

11 print (func(-2))
```

[Code Description]

In lines 4, 6 and 8, a variable result is added to record the status of program branches through assignment statements. The ninth line of code returns the value of result, so that the result of each branch can be returned by calling the same return statement.

Nesting of functions

Nesting of functions refers to calling other functions inside a function. C and C++ only allow nesting within function bodies, while Python not only supports nesting within function bodies but also supports nesting of function definitions. For example, calculate the value of expression (one+two)*(first-second). The calculation step can be divided into three steps: first, calculate the expression one+two, then calculate the expression first-second, and finally calculate the product of the results of the first two steps. Therefore, the three functions can be designed. The first function sum () calculates the value of one+two, the second function sub () calculates the value of m+n, and the third function calculates the product of the first two.

The following code demonstrates the calling operation between functions.

```
01 # nested function
02 def sum(add, sub):
03 return add+sub
04 def sub(add, sub):
05 return add-sub
06 def function():
07 ex=1
```

```
08 ey=2

09 em=3

10 en=4

11 return sum(ex, ey) * sub(em, en)

13 print (function())
```

[Code Description]

The second line of code defines the function sum (), sum () with two parameters a and b. Parameters a and b are used to calculate the value of expression x+y.

The code in line 3 calculates the value of a+b, that is, returns the result of X+Y.

The fourth line of code defines the function sub (), sub () with two parameters a and b.

The code in line 5 calculates the value of a−b, i.e., returns the result of m−n.

The 11th line of code calls sum (), sub (), and performs multiplication in the return statement.

Line 13 code, call function function ().

The output is shown below:

-3

Note that the number of nesting levels of functions should not be too high. Otherwise, it is easy to cause problems such as poor readability and difficult maintenance of the code. Nested calls to general functions should be controlled within 3 levels.

The above code can also be implemented in another form, i.e., the functions sum () and sub () are placed inside func ().

The following code implements the definition of sum (), sub () inside function ().

01 # nested function

02 def function():

03 ex=1

04 yov=2

05 men=3

06 nod=4

07 def sum(am, bam): # internal function

08 return am+bam

09 def sub(am, bam): # internal function

10 return am-bam

11 return sum(ex, yov) * sub(am, bn)

13 print (function())

[Code Description]

In line 7, sum () is defined inside function ().

Line 9 code defines sub () inside function ().

Line 11 code, call sum () and sub () and then perform multiplication. The output is "-3."

Internal functions sum (), sub () can also directly call variables defined by external function function ().

The following code implements the variables of the internal function sum (), sub () that refer to the external function function ().

01 # nested function, directly using the variable

02 def function () of the outer function:

03 first= 1

04 second = 2

05 third = 3

06 fourth = 4

```
07 def sum(): # internal function

08 return first + second

09 def sub(): # internal function

10 return third - fourth

11 return sum() * sub()

13 print (function())
```

[Code Description]

In line 7, the function sum () has no parameters.

Line 8 code calls external variables x, y inside sum ().

In line 9, the function sub () also has no arguments.

Line 10 code calls external variables m, n inside sub ().

Line 11 code, calculate the value of sum()*sub (). The output result is "-3"

Be careful not to define functions inside them.

This method is not easy to maintain the program, and it is easy to cause logical confusion. Moreover, the more levels of nested definition functions, the higher the cost of program maintenance.

Recursive functions

Recursive functions can call themselves directly or indirectly within the function body, that is, the nesting of functions is the function itself. Recursion is a program design method. Recursion can reduce repeated codes and make the program concise. The process of recursion is divided into two stages-recursion and regression. The principle of the recursive function is as follows.

In the first stage, recursive functions call themselves internally. Each function call restarts executing the code of the function until a certain level of the recursive program ends.

In the second stage, recursive functions return from back to forth. Recursive functions return from the last level until they are returned to the function body called for the first time. That is, after the recursion step-by-step call is completed, it returns step-by-step in the reverse order.

Note that recursive functions need to write conditions for recursion to end; otherwise, the recursive program will not end. Generally, the program is ended by judging the statement.

Calculating factorial is a classical recursive implementation. First of all, review the calculation formula of factorial.

For example, calculate 5! As a result when designing a program, one can judge whether n is equal to 1. Each recursive call passes in parameter n-1. Until n=1, returns 1! is equal to 1. Then return to 2! 、 3! 、 4! 、 5!

Process of calculating factorials using recursion

The following code recursively implements the factorial calculation process.

01 # Calculates factorial

02 def refund(n):

03 one = 1

04 if second > 1: # end judgment of recursion

05 one = n

06 true = true * refund(n-1) # recursion

07 print ("%d! =" %i, n)

08 return n # return

09

10 refund(5)

[Code Description]

The second line of code defines a recursive function. The definition of a recursive function is no different from that of an ordinary function. The third line of code defines a variable I for the output of the print statement.

Line 4 code is used to judge the passed parameter n. If n is greater than 1, the function can continue recursion. Otherwise, the result of the current calculation is returned.

The fifth line of code assigns the value of n to I and uses I to record the current recursive number.

Line 6 calls function refunc () itself, passing parameter n-1. The seventh line of code outputs the result of the factorial calculation.

The eighth line of code returns the calculation result of factorial of each level.

Line 10 calls the recursive function refund.

The output of each recursion is as follows:

1! =1

2! =2

3! =6

4! =24

5! =120

Note that every time a recursive function is called, all variables in the function will be copied before the recursive function is executed. The program needs more storage space, which will affect the performance of the program to some extent. Therefore, it is better to use other methods to improve programs that do not need recursion.

You can use the aforementioned reduce () to quickly implement factorial operations.

01 # Calculates factorial with reduce

02 from func tools import reduce # python3 reduce is no longer in the global, must be manually introduced

03 print ("5! =," reduce(lambda x, y: x * y, range(1, 6)))

Using reduce () requires only one line of code to calculate 5!.

Lambda function

Lambda function is used to create an anonymous function whose name is not bound to the identifier. Using lambda function can return some simple operation results.

Lambda functions have the following format:

Lambda variable 1, variable 2 ...: expression

Among them, the variable list is used for expression calculation. Lambda belongs to a function, so a colon is required after the variable list. Lambda is usually assigned to a variable, which can be used as a function.

For example:

01 # assignment

02 function=lambda variable 1, variable 2 ...: expression

Call

04 function()

This binds lambda and variable function, whose name is the function name. Lambda function can eliminate internal functions.

For example, the program for calculating (one+two) * (three−nfour) in subsection can be modified to replace the functions sum (), sub () with lambda functions.

01 # lambda

02 def func():

03 one = 1

04 two = 2

05 three= 3

06 four = 4

```
07 sum = lambda one, two : one + two

08 print (sum)

09 sub = lambda three, four : three - four

10 print (sub)

11 return sum(one, two) * sub(three, four)

13 print (function())
```

[Code description]

Line 7 defines the lambda function, realizes the calculation expression first+second, and assigns the lambda function to the variable sum.

The eighth line of code outputs the value of the variable sum, which holds the address of the lambda function.

The output is shown below:

<function <lambda> at 0x00B4D3B0>

Lines 9 and 10 have the same function as lines 7 and 8.

Line 11 calculates the product of sum () and sub (). The output is "-3."

Note that lambda is also called an expression. Only expressions can be used in lambda, and multiple statements such as judgment and loop cannot be used. In the previous example, lambda is assigned to a variable and can also be used directly as a function.

Function usage of lambda

01 # lambda

02 print ((lambda first: -first)(-2))

[Code Description]

The code in line 2 defines the anonymous function lambda x: -x, which is used to return the absolute value of a number. The parameter of the function is -2, and the output result is "2."

By this, we have discussed in detail about functions and modules that are important for software development using python. We will, in the next chapter, discuss about object-oriented concepts in detail.

Chapter 6: Object-oriented Programming in Python

This chapter will describe object-oriented concepts in python in detail with examples. This is important for a better understanding of the robustness of the python language and the opportunities it gives. We will go through concepts like classes and objects in detail. Let us dive into it in a detailed mode.

What Is Object-Oriented Programming?

Object-oriented technology is an important technology in the field of software engineering. This kind of software development idea naturally simulates human's understanding of the objective world and has become the mainstream of computer software engineering at present.

Python, as an object-oriented computer programming language, it is very important to master the idea of object-oriented programming. Therefore, we have arranged two chapters to explain it. We hope that through the study of these two chapters, everyone can establish the idea of object-oriented programming and learn to use this idea to develop programs.

Overview of Object-Oriented Programming

There are various forms of things in the real world, and there are various connections between these things. In the program, objects are used to map real things, and the relationships between objects are used to describe the relationships between things. This idea is object-oriented.

When we talk about object-oriented, we naturally think of process-oriented. Process-oriented is to analyze the steps to solve the problem, and then use functions to implement these steps one by one, one by one when using.

Object-oriented is to decompose the problem-solving things into multiple objects, and the purpose of establishing objects is not to complete one step by one but to describe the behavior of one thing in the process of solving the whole problem. The following is an example of gobang to illustrate the difference between process-oriented and object-oriented programming.

First, use process-oriented:

1. Start the game.

2. Sunspots go first

3. Draw the picture

4. Judging winning or losing

5. It's Bai Zi's turn

6. Draw the picture

7. Judging winning or losing

8. Return to Step 2

9. Output Final Results

The above steps are implemented by functions, respectively, and the problem is solved.

Object-oriented design is to solve the problem from another way of thinking. When using object-oriented thinking to realize gobang, the whole gobang can be divided into three types of objects, as follows.

1. Black and white parties: the two parties behave the same

2. Chessboard system: responsible for drawing pictures

3. Rule system: responsible for judging such things as foul, winning or losing, etc.

Among the above three-class objects, the first-class object (black and white parties) is responsible for receiving the user's input and notifying the second-class object (chessboard system) to draw pieces on the chessboard, while the third-class object (rule system) judges the chessboard.

Object-oriented ensures the unity of functions, thus making the code easier to maintain. For example, if we want to add the function of regret chess now, then a series of steps of input, judgment, and display needs to be changed, even the loops between steps need to be adjusted on a large scale, which is obviously very troublesome.

If object-oriented development is used, only the chessboard object needs to be changed. The chessboard object saves the chessboard scores of both black and white parties, only needs simple backtracking, and the display and rules do not need to be changed. At the same time, the calling sequence of the whole object function will not change, and its changes are only partial. Thus, compared with process-oriented, object-oriented programming is more convenient for later code maintenance and function expansion.

Categories and Objects

In object-oriented programming, the two most important core concepts are class and object. Objects are concrete things in real life. They can be seen and touched. For example, the book you are holding is an object.

Compared with objects, classes are abstract, which is a general designation for a group of things with the same characteristics and behaviors. For example, when I was a child, my mother said to you, "Son, you should take that kind of person as an example!" The type of people here refers to a group of people who have excellent academic results and are polite. They have the same characteristics, so they are called "type" people.

Relationship between class and object

As the saying goes, "people are grouped by category, and things are grouped by group," we collectively refer to the collection of things with similar characteristics and behaviors as categories, such as animals, airplanes, etc. Class is an abstract description of a certain kind of thing, while the object is an individual of this kind of thing in reality.

Relationship between classes and objects

The toy model can be regarded as a class and each toy as an object. Thus, the relationship between the toy model and the toy can be regarded as the relationship between the class and the object. Class is used to describe the common features of multiple objects and is a template for objects. The object is used to describe individuals in reality. It is an instance of a class. As can be seen from the examples, objects are created according to classes, and one class can correspond to multiple objects.

Definition of category

In daily life, to describe a kind of thing, it is necessary to explain its characteristics as well as its uses. For example, when describing such things as human beings, it is usually necessary to give a definition or name to such things. Human characteristics include height, weight, sex, occupation, etc. Human behaviors include running, speaking, etc.

The combination of human characteristics and behaviors can completely describe human beings. The design idea of an object-oriented program is based on this design, which includes the features and behaviors of things in classes. Among them, the characteristics of things are taken as the attributes of classes, the behaviors of things are taken as the methods of classes, and objects are an instance of classes.

So, to create an object, you need to define a class first. Class is composed of 3 parts.

(1) Class Name: The name of the class, whose initial letter must be uppercase, such as Person.

(2) Attributes: used to describe the characteristics of things, such as people's names, ages, etc.

(3) Method: Used to describe the behavior of things; for example, people have behaviors such as talking and smiling.

In Python, you can use the class keyword to declare a class with the following basic syntax format:

Class classname:

The property of the class

Method of class

The following is a sample code:

class Ox:

attribute

Method

```
def eat(grass):
```

Print ("-eating grass--")

In the above example, the class is used to define a class named Ox, in which there is an eat method. As can be seen from the example, the format of the method is the same as that of the function. The main difference is that the method must explicitly declare a self-parameter and be located at the beginning of the parameter list. Self represents the instance of the class (object) itself, which can be used to refer to the attributes and methods of the object. The specific usage of self will be introduced later with practical application.

Creating objects from classes

If a program wants to complete specific functions, classes alone are not enough, and instance objects need to be created according to classes. In Python programs, you can use the following syntax to create an object:

Object Name = ClassName ()

For example, create an object Ox of Ox class with the following sample code:

Ox= Ox()

In the above code, Ox is actually a variable that can be used to access the properties and methods of the class. To add attributes to an object, you can:

Object Name. New Attribute Name = Value. For example, use cat to add the color attribute to an object of Cat class.

The sample code is as follows:

Ox.color = "white"

Next, a complete case is used to demonstrate how to create objects, add attributes, and call methods.

Example helicopter.py

1 # Define Class

2   class Helicopter:

3 # move

4   def fly(autom):

5   print (" Helicopter Running ..."

6 # honking

7   def toot(autom):

8   print ("the plane is honking ... beeping ...")

9 # creates an object and saves its reference with the variable JB23

10 Jb23 = Flight()

11 # Add Attribute Representing Color

12 JB23.color = "black"

13 # Call Method

14 JB23.move()

15 JB23.toot()

16 # Access Attributes

17 print(JB23.color)

In the example, a Plane class is defined, two methods move, and toot are defined in the class, then an object JB23 of Plane class is created, color attribute is dynamically added and assigned to "black," then move () and toot () methods are called in turn, and the value of color attribute is printed out.

Structural Methods and Destructural Methods

In Python programs, two special methods are provided: __init__ () and __del__ (), which are respectively used to initialize the properties of the object and release the resources occupied by the class. This section mainly introduces these two methods in detail.

Construction method

In the case of a section, we dynamically added the color attribute to the objects referenced by JB23. Just imagine, if you create another Plane class object, you need to add attributes in the form of "object name.attribute name." For each object you create, you need to add attributes once, which is obviously very troublesome.

To solve this problem, attributes can be set when creating an object. Python provides a construction method with a fixed name of __init__ (two underscores begin and two underscores end). When creating an instance of a class, the system will automatically call the constructor to initialize the class.

In order to make everyone better understand, the following is a case to demonstrate how to use the construction method for initialization.

to define the class

2   class Plane:

```
3 # construction method

4      def __init__(autom):

Color = "black"

6 # honking

7      def toot(autom):

8 print ("%s plane is honking ..." (autom.color))

9 # creates an object and saves its reference with the variable
plane

10 plane = Plane()

No.11 plane honked

12 plane.toot()
```

These lines re-implemented the __init__ () method, adding the color attribute to the Plane class and assigning it a value of "black," and accessing the value of the color attribute in the toot method.

Operation results

No matter how many Plane objects are created, the initial value of the color attribute is "black" by default. If you want to modify the default value of the property after the object is created, you can set the value of the property by passing parameters in the construction method. The following is a case to demonstrate how to use the construction method with parameters, as shown.

Example uses the parametric construction method. py

1 # Define Class

2   class Plane:

3 # belt parameter construction method

4   def __init__(autom, color):

Color = color6 # honking

7   def toot(autom):

8 print ("%s color plane honking ..." %autom.color)

9 # creates an object and saves its reference with the variable JB23

10 JB23 = Plane ("Snow White")

11 # creates an object and saves its reference with variable ferrari

12 ferrari = Plane ("red")

No.13 plane honked

14 JB23.toot()

15 ferrari.toot()

In examples, lines 4 to 5 customize the construction method with parameters and assign the value of the parameters to the color attribute to ensure that the value of the color attribute changes with the value received by the parameters, and then it is still accessed in the toot method.

Destructural methods

Earlier, we introduced the __init__ () method. When an object is created, the Python interpreter will call the __init__ () method by default. When deleting an object to release the resources occupied by the class, the Python interpreter calls another method by default, which is the __del__ () method.

Next, a case is used to demonstrate how to use destructor to release the occupied resources, as shown.

Example uses the destructor. py

```
# Define Class

class Person:

    def __init__(autom, name, age):

        autom.name = name

        autom.love = love

    def __del__(autom):
```

Print ("-del----") laowang = person ("Lao Wang," 30)

In the example, a class named Person is defined, the initial values of name and age are set in the __init__ () method, a print statement is added in the __del__ () method, and then an object of the Person class is created using a custom construction method.

Thus we have given a brief introduction to object-oriented programming in this chapter. In the next chapter, we will discuss Files in python in detail. Come along with us to enjoy the final chapter of this book.

Chapter 7: Files in Python

This chapter will give a brief introduction to files in python. We will have various examples that will help us understand the files, their structure, and implementation.

What are Files in Python?

The data can be stored using either a database or a file. The database maintains the integrity and relevance of the data and makes the data safer and more reliable. Using files to store data is very simple and easy to use, and there is no need to install database management systems and other operating environments.

Files are usually used to store application software parameters or temporary data. Python's file operation is very similar to Java's file operation. Python provides modules such as os and os.path to process files.

Files and streams

Common Operation of Files

Files are usually used to store data or application system parameters. Python provides os, os.path, shutil, and other modules to process files, including functions such as opening files, reading and writing files, copying and deleting files.

Creation of Files

In Python3, the global file () function has been removed, and the open () function has been retained. The function open () can be used to open or create files. This function can specify the processing mode and set the open file to read-only, write-only, or read-write status.

The declaration of open () is as follows:

open(file, mode='r', buffering=-1, encoding=None,

errors=None, newline=None, closefd=Trueopener=None) -> file object

[Code Description]

The parameter file is the name of the opened file. If the file does not exist, open () creates a file named name and then opens the file. The parameter mode refers to the open mode of the file. Parameter buffering sets the cache mode. 0 means no cache; 1 indicates line buffering. If it is greater than 1, it indicates the size of the buffer, in bytes.

Here, open () returns a file object, which can perform various operations on the file.

Opening Mode of Files notes that "B" mode must be used for reading and writing files such as pictures and videos.

The file class is used for file management. It can create, open, read and write, close files, etc.

File processing is generally divided into the following 3 steps:

1) Create and open a file and use the file () function to return a file object.

2) Call read (), write () and other methods of the file object to process the file.

3) Call close () to close the file and release the resources occupied by the file object.

Note that the close () method is necessary. Although Python provides a garbage collection mechanism to clean up objects that are no longer used, it is a good habit to manually release resources that are no longer needed. It also explicitly tells Python's garbage collector that the object needs to be cleaned.

The following code demonstrates the creation, writing, and closing of files.

01 # Create File

02 context='''This is countryside'''

03 f=open('rod.txt', 'w') # open file

04 f.write(context) # write string to file

Close () # close file

[Code Description]

The third line of code calls open () to create the file hello.txt and sets the access mode of the file to "W." Open () returns file object f.

The fourth line of code writes the value of the variable context into the file hello.txt

Line 5 calls the close () method of object f to release the resources occupied by object f.

These three steps will also be followed in the operations of reading, writing, deleting, and copying files explained later.

Reading of files

There are many ways to read a file. You can use readline (), readlines (), or Read () functions to read a file. The implementation method of reading files by these functions will be introduced one by one.

1. readline ()

Readline () reads one line of the file at a time, and the file needs to be read cyclically using a permanent true expression. However, when the file pointer moves to the end of the file, there will be an error reading the file using readline (). Therefore, a judgment statement needs to be added to the program to judge whether the file pointer moves to the end of the file, and the loop is interrupted by the statement. The following code demonstrates the use of readline ().

```
01 # Use readline () to Read Files

02 f=open("rod.txt")

03 while True:

04 line=f.readline()

05 if line:

06 print (line)

07 else:

08 break

09 f.close()
```

[Code Description]

The code in line 3 uses "True" as the loop condition to form a permanent true loop.

Line 4 calls readline () to read every line of the hello.txt file. Each cycle outputs the following results in turn.

This is countryside

Line 5 code, judge whether the variable LINE is true. If true, the content of the current line is output; otherwise, exit the loop. If the fourth line of code is changed to the following statement, the reading method is slightly different, but the reading content is exactly the same.

line=f.readline(2)

This line of code does not mean that only 2 bytes are read per line, but that each line reads 2 bytes at a time until the end of the line.

2. Multi-line reading method readlines ()

To read a file using readlines (), you need to return the elements in the list by looping through readlines (). The readlines () function reads multiple lines of data in a file at once.

The following code demonstrates how readlines () reads a file.

```
01 # use readlines () to read files

02 f=file('rod.txt')

03 lines=f.readlines()

04 for line in lines: # read multiple lines at once

05 print (line)

06 f.close()
```

[Code Description]

The third line of code calls readlines () to store all the contents of the file rod.txt in the list lines.

The fourth line of code loops through the contents of the list lines.

Line 5 code output list lines for each element

```
01 f=open("rod.txt")

02 context=f.read(5) # reads the first 5 bytes of the file

03 print (context)

04 print (f.tell()) # returns the current pointer position of the
file object

05 context=f.read(5) # continue reading 5 bytes of content

06 print (context)

07 print (f.tell()) # output file current pointer position

08 f.close()
```

[Code Description]

The second line of code calls read(5) to read the contents of the first 5 bytes in the hello.txt file and store it in the variable context. At this point, the pointer of the file moves to the 5th byte.

The third line of code outputs the result of the variable context and the output is "hello."

Line 4 calls tell () to output the current file

Line 5 code calls read(5) again to read the contents of bytes 6 to 10.

The output of line 6 is "world."

Line 7 code outputs the current file pointer position: 10.

Note that the location of the file pointer will be recorded inside the file object for the next operation. As long as the file object does not execute the close () method, the file pointer will not be released.

Writing of files

The implementation of file writing also has many methods. You can use the write (), writelines () methods to write files. It uses the write () method to write strings to files, while the writelines () method can write the contents stored in the list to files.

The following code demonstrates how to write elements in the list to a file.

01 # use writelines () to write files

```
02 f=file("rod.txt," "w+")

03 li=["hello country side\n," "hello city\n"]

04 f.writelines(li)

05 f.close()
```

[Code Description]

The second line of code uses the "w+" mode to create and open the file hello.txt

Line 3 defines a list Li. Li stores 2 elements, each representing 1 line in the file, and "\n" is used for line feed.

The fourth line of code calls writelines () to write the contents of list li into the file.

The contents of the document are as follows.

hello countryside

hello City

The above two methods will erase the original contents of the file before writing and rewrite the new contents, which is equivalent to "overwriting." If you need to keep the original contents of the file and just add new contents, you can open the file using mode "a+."

The following code demonstrates the join operation of the file.

```
01 # Joins New Content to File

02 f=file("rod.txt," "first+") # is written by joining a+

03 new_context="It is over"

04 f.write(getdetails)

05 f.close()
```

[Code Description]

The second line of code uses the mode "first+" to open the file hello.txt

The fourth line of code calls the write () method, the original contents of the hello.txt file remain unchanged, and the contents of the variable getdetails are written to the end of the rod.txt file. Txt is as follows.

hello countryside

hello City

goodbye

Writing files using writelines () is faster. If there are too many strings to write to a file, you can use writelines () to improve efficiency. If only a small number of strings need to be written, write () can be used directly.

Deletion of documents

The deletion of files requires the use of os modules and os.path modules. Os module provides operating system-level interface functions for system environment, files, directories, etc. File Handling Functions Commonly Used in os Modules Note that the use of the OS module's open () function is different from that of the built-in open () function.

The removal of the file needs to be implemented by calling the remove () function. Before deleting a file, it is necessary to determine whether the file exists or not, if so, delete the file; otherwise, nothing will be done.

The following code demonstrates the deletion of the file:

01 import os

03 file("rod.txt," "w")

04 if os.path.exists("rod.txt"):

05 os.remove("rod.txt")

[Code Description]

Line 3 code creates the file hello.txt

The fourth line of code calls the existing () of os.path module to determine whether the file hello.txt exists.

Line 5 calls remove () to delete the file hello.txt

Reproduction of documents

The file class does not provide a method for directly copying files, but the read () and write () methods can be used to copy files. The following code copies the contents of hello.txt to hello2.txt.

```
01 # uses read (), write () to copy

Txt

03 src=file("rod.txt," "w")

04 li=["hello world\n," "hello US\n"]

05 src.writelines(li)

06 src.close()

07 # copy rod.txt to rod2.txt

08 src=open("rod.txt," "r")

09 dst=open("rod2.txt," "w")

10 dst.write(src.read())

11 src.close()

12 dst.close()
```

[Code Description]

Line 8 code opens the file hello.txt as read-only.

Line 9 code opens the file hello2.txt in a write-only manner.

In line 10, read () the contents of hello.txt, and then write these contents into rod2.txt. Shutil module is another file and directory management interface, providing some functions for copying files and directories. Copyfile () function can copy files.

The declaration of copyfile () function is as follows:

copyfile(src, dst)

[Code Description]

The parameter src represents the path of the source file and src is a string type.

The parameter dst represents the path of the target file, and dst is a string type.

This function copies the file pointed to by src to the file pointed to by dst.

The file can be cut using the move () function, which is declared as follows.

copyfile(src, dst, *, follow_symlinks=True)

The parameter of move () is the same as copyfile (), move A file or directory is moved to a specified location, and the moved file can be renamed according to the parameter dst. The following code uses shutil module to copy files.

01 # shutil Module Implements File Replication

02 import shutil

03

04 shutil.copyfile("rod.txt,""rod2.txt")

05 shutil.move("rod.txt,".",/")

06 shutil.move("rod2.txt,""rod3.txt")

[Code Description]

The fourth line of code calls copyfile (), copying the contents of hello.txt to hello2.txt.

Line 5 calls move (), copies hello.txt to the parent directory of the current directory, and then deletes hello.txt. Txt and paste it into the parent directory.

Line 6 calls move () to move hello2.txt to the current directory and name it hello3.txt. Txt will be deleted.

Renaming of files

The function rename () of the os module can rename files or directories. The following code demonstrates the file renaming operation. If there is a file named hello.txt in the current directory, rename it hi.txt; if there is a hi.txt file, rename it hello.txt.

```
01 # Modify File Name

02 import os

03 li=os.listdir(.”")

04 print (li)

05 if "hello.txt" in li:

06 os.rename("hello.txt," "hi.txt")

07 elif "hi.txt" in li:

08 os.rename("hi.txt," "hello.txt")
```

[Code Description]

The third line of code calls listdir () to return the file list of the current directory, where .”" indicates the current directory.

Thus, we have ended this book that explained a lot of python topics in detail with the help of various examples. This is enough to start a small-medium-level project which can help you implement all these concepts. Use GitHub to find different python projects and start reading them. All the best for your Coding Career. Cheers!

Conclusion

Thank you for making it through to the end of *Python for beginners*. Let's hope it was informative and able to provide you with all of the tools you need to achieve your goals whatever they may be.

The next step is to implement these concepts to build coding projects and software applications. We have discussed a lot of concepts from basics to advanced stuff in detail.

Finally, if you found this book useful in any way, a review on Amazon is always appreciated!

www.ingramcontent.com/pod-product-compliance
Lightning Source LLC
Chambersburg PA
CBHW052140070326
40690CB00047B/1249